WATER CONFIDENTIAL

Caitlin Press Inc.
3375 Ponderosa Way
Qualicum Beach, BC V9K 2J8
www.caitlinpress.com

Text and cover design by Vici Johnstone
Edited by Holly Vestad
Printed in Canada

All images from the author's personal collection.

Caitlin Press Inc. acknowledges financial support from the Government of Canada and the Canada Council for the Arts, and the Province of British Columbia through the British Columbia Arts Council and the Book Publisher's Tax Credit.

Library and Archives Canada Cataloguing in Publication

Water confidential : witnessing justice denied -- the fight for safe drinking water in
  Indigenous and rural communities in Canada / by Susan Blacklin.
Blacklin, Susan, author.
Includes bibliographical references.
Canadiana 20230525334 | ISBN 9781773861319 (softcover)
LCSH: Water-supply—Canada. | LCSH: Right to water—Canada. | LCSH: Drinking water—
  Government policy—Canada. | LCSH: Drinking water—Standards—Canada. | LCSH: Water
quality management—Canada. | LCSH: Indigenous peoples—Health and hygiene—Canada.
| LCSH: Indigenous peoples—Canada—Government relations. | LCSH: Blacklin, Susan. |
LCSH: Human rights workers—Canada—Biography. | LCGFT: Autobiographies.
Classification: LCC HD1696.C2 B53 2024 | DDC 363.6/108997071—dc23

WATER
CONFIDENTIAL

Witnessing Justice Denied—

The Fight for Safe Drinking Water in Indigenous and
Rural Communities in Canada

SUSAN BLACKLIN

Caitlin Press 2024

This book is dedicated to all Indigenous communities and all Canadians. May we one day all benefit from national drinking water regulations.

Contents

Glossary of Acronyms

BWA	Boil Water Advisory
INAC	Indigenous and Northern Affairs Canada
NRC	National Research Council
OWD	Operation Water Drop
SDWF	Safe Drinking Water Foundation
SFNWA	Saskatchewan First Nations Water Association
SRC	Saskatchewan Research Council
WHO	World Health Organization
WRC	WateResearch Corporation

These are my memories of events and my emotions. Others' memories may vary, or they may have experienced different emotions.

Foreword by Erin Poochay

Yellow Quill First Nation

I moved on Reserve when I was seven, in 1990. In those days we still collected rain water, gathered snow to melt and collected water from sloughs to drink. I grew up conserving water, valuing it by not wasting. Fast forward to my pre-teens. We had water tanks for our homes, for washing and indoor plumbing. We still didn't drink the tap water. I remember it was yellow and left stains in our sinks and toilet. I began to have skin problems. I had eczema on both hands, and it would periodically get infected, affecting my attendance at school and sports. My late mother, Greta Slippery, was a band councillor at the time (four consecutive terms from 1991 to 1999) and I remember she kept taking me to the doctor and wanted me to see a dermatologist. Retrospectively I like to believe she and other community members searched for resources and allies to improve our water. The women were the home keepers and knew what was needed—we needed clean drinking water. Water that we could wash in that wouldn't cause skin sores and infections. I don't know or remember the timeline of events that led to the community getting a state of the art water treatment system, but I do remember bottled water was provided to each household. And there were talks of a waterline going through the community. It was exciting to wash in water that wasn't yellow and do laundry at home. When we did get the waterline, it's like we still didn't trust drinking from the tap for some time. We continued getting bottled water; but eventually we did drink from the tap. Currently I am a Band Councillor. Over the years I have worked for the band in various capacities, including research. Listening to Traditional Knowledge Keepers and Elders talk about our water, I have learned that some (I have still so much to learn) of my understanding is theirs too. Water is so sacred, and the value of it is honoured in our traditional teachings. When I was approached to write this I wanted to make sure the record showed that the whole community came together in various capacities to get proper water treatment. I recently had a conversation with our current chief, John Machiskinic. "You used to be able to drink water from anywhere." He talked about how over time the water became contaminated from farming chemicals, and how much work it was to haul drinking water. When Chief Machiskinic spoke about water today, he said, "...everything is so easy. There's a tap, and washing machines. I have read the articles of Peterson's findings, and understand what kind of work goes into researching these projects. He honoured us by using his reputation, time and expertise to help; for that we are grateful."

Foreword by Dr. John O'Connor

Family Physician, and passionate Health Advocate,
Northern Alberta, a thorn in the side of Health Canada,
Government of Alberta, and the Tar Sands

Susan (Sue) Blacklin has a particular insight into the challenges associated with provision, supply and maintenance of clean, dependable water, especially in Indigenous communities in Canada.

Along with her late eminent husband Hans Peterson, Sue was very much in the trenches in the struggle to ensure that a basic source of consumable water was available for the most needy and ignored communities. In *Water Confidential*, Sue has written a hard-hitting, from-the-heart description of the lengths taken, obstacles overcome, and sacrifices made, along what was an extraordinary, meandering path to establish access to the source of life in the setting of gross neglect and overt discrimination. That Hans and Sue had to undertake what they did is an indictment of Canada's attitude to Indigenous communities, even when it comes to basic human rights.

Unfortunately, the story and struggle are far from over. So many water contaminants are still not being assessed. Case in point—the constant seepage/leakage/government-sanctioned discharges from the nineteen (and counting) tar sands tailing impoundments full of toxin-laden "process" water in northern Alberta. These "ponds" connect directly and indirectly to the Athabasca River, and by industry and government admissions are designed and engineered to leak. They lie upstream of Indigenous communities and precious wetlands. Sampling of river and surface water occurs at distances from toxin entry points—and in circumstances dictated by self-monitored, government-supported industry. Remember, the Alberta Energy Regulator charged with policing oil industry activities is financed by the oil industry. While there is little acknowledgement that some tailings water chemicals are of concern, safe exposure limits utilized are generous and not at all in keeping with WHO guidelines. There is also no attention paid to the toxic "soup" resulting from the mix of these hazardous materials—the handling of which frequently requires use of PPE on industrial sites. Independent respected scientific analysis confirms some of the toxins are Endocrine Disruptors, and have been shown to enter the food chain, impacting fish embryos, for instance. Downstream communities traditionally live off the water and land exposed to these chemicals for decades. They see the results of upstream industrial activity but cannot get their concerns heard. Traditional Environmental Knowledge has long borne witness to these changes. Human health impacts seem to be on the rise—curiously never formally studied, despite many recommendations. This information is definitely not new, but triggers no alarm bells, other than in those communities, for the health and safety of those at risk. This constitutes active ecocide and, unfortunately, genocide.

Alberta is certainly not alone in Canada when it comes to situations such as this.

The term "Boil Water Advisory" is increasingly a misnomer. This generally applies to water that may harbour pathogenic micro-organisms. However, no amount of boiling will clear *this* chemical burden. In addition to consumption, bathing in such contaminated water is often ill-advised and the subject of warnings. A more accurate term surely is "Water Safety Advisory"—though that would/will have much wider implications for issuing authorities.

In reality, until Traditional Environmental Knowledge gets the respect it deserves from Conventional Environmental Knowledge, we will not make the kind of progress that counts. The establishment and maintenance of a universal safe and secure water supply requires honesty, integrity, impartiality and unconditional commitment on all sides.

Until water ceases to be a commodity—not anytime soon unfortunately—there's little hope for that.

Foreword by Warren Goulding

Author of *Just Another Indian: A Serial Killer*
and Canada's Indifference

The United Nations has declared that the provision of safe, affordable water is a basic human right. Through a 2010 resolution, the United Nations General Assembly recognized the human right to clean water and sanitation and stated that the "human right to water is indispensable for leading a life in human dignity. It is a prerequisite for the realization of other human rights."[1]

Sadly, that right has not been respected over many generations for residents of Indigenous communities in Canada who have been denied access to acceptable drinking water.

It is a national disgrace; another ignominy in a colonial history that has brought shame to Canada on the international stage. And it has led to decades of disease, financial hardship and anxiety for people living on reserves throughout Canada.

Among the cruel ironies of this deplorable situation is the fact that Canada's water quality is considered among the best in the world. However, dozens of First Nations communities continue to struggle with the challenge of providing safe water for their members.

Susan Blacklin has been on the frontlines of the campaign to bring safe drinking water to First Nations communities, working closely with her late husband, Dr. Hans Peterson, a renowned scientist, and the founder of the Safe Drinking Water Foundation. Dr. Peterson pioneered the development of the Integrated Biological and Reverse Osmosis Membrane water treatment process. In a tribute to Dr. Peterson, who died in 2018, Nicole Hancock, executive director of the Safe Drinking Water Foundation, said, "There's over 100,000 people who have safe drinking water because of Peterson's invention. Even after he retired, he was working eighteen-hour days trying to push water issues forward."[2] Indeed, it was a monumental commitment to a cause that Peterson pursued with a selfless passion.

Beginning in 1996, Susan acknowledges the toll the work exacted on their family was unmistakable in terms of finances and daily life that was rife with frustrations and disappointments.

Looking back on a period of twenty-five years, Susan celebrates the accomplishments, but pulls no punches in exposing the indifference, incompetence, and corruption on the part of governments at all levels in the name of providing safe drinking water for Indigenous communities.

Water Confidential is an unabashed, insider's perspective of a vital work in progress, one that continues to this day as dozens of communities continue to search for solutions to their water problems. There has been progress, but decades of hollow promises and inaction have not produced solutions for a largely marginalized population that continues to live with boil water advisories and threats to their health.

"While water quality and water-borne disease are often a greater concern in developing nations, a water-borne disease burden exists in developed nations. There are an estimated 20.5 million episodes of enteric disease in Canada each year (Thomas *et al.* 2013), of which, over 400,000 are estimated to be related to drinking water (Murphy *et al.* 2016a, 2016b)."

From: *Drinking and recreational water exposures among Canadians: Foodbook Study 2014–2015*, authors: Rachelle Janicki; M. Kate Thomas; Katarina Pintar; Manon Fleury; Andrea Nesbitt https://iwaponline.com/jwh/article/16/2/197/38000/Drinking-and-recreational-water-exposures-among

Prologue

Hans and I were adopted into the Indigenous culture of the Saddle Lake Cree Nation by one of its councillors, Elder Howard Cardinal, in the summer of 2006. The community invited Hans and me to be guests of honour in their Sweat Lodge ceremony to commemorate our work. The community held a pipe ceremony to honour the water spirit. The ceremony was the most beautiful and humbling experience.

Six peace pipes were lit and handed around to all participants. The Elders had a specific chant as the pipe was passed to each person. The "sweat" is a canvas hut inside a log building on a gravel floor. Outside, a large fire was started. Layers of stones, about ten inches in diameter, were stacked alternately with layers of logs. The leaders carefully carried the stones into the sweat on pitchforks as the stones became red hot.

Inside the tent was a centre pit where they positioned the red-hot stones. Fourteen stones were brought in—one each for the fourteen elders present—and the canvas flap was closed. The temperature quickly rose. Then, the chanting began.

The chanting reminded me of singing "Ten Green Bottles" when I was young, or songs we sang at soccer matches or on school bus rides. A powerful spirit is evoked from communal chanting; combined with the cultural practices of the Saddle Lake Cree, the experience was riveting. The many hours we had tirelessly toiled and our dedication to helping Indigenous communities were worthwhile; their genuine appreciation was overwhelming. Afterwards, we went for a lunch of moose stew and bannock. Then, two men took an offering of tobacco in a canoe out to the lake for the water spirit.

The Yellow Quill community also held an appreciation ceremony for Hans and me, and we were deeply touched. The community gave us each an eagle feather while they burned sweetgrass, announcing that while they appreciated Hans's commitment to help First Nations people, they also appreciated the support I had given them. The entire community chanted and clapped.

An Elder in the community made us two Indigenous quilts hand-sewn with love. The people wrapped one around each of us, and we felt their love and appreciation to our core, bringing us both to tears. Later, I took the feathers and sweetgrass to an Indigenous artist, Ernie Scoles. He mounted them in a large, framed picture and tied the two eagle feathers with the sweetgrass. That framed picture still hangs in our daughter's bedroom today.

Introduction

I rarely watch television, but in 2023 I noticed a commercial encouraging First Nations, Métis and Inuit people who have lived with a boil water advisory (BWA) for a year or more to sign up for a class action lawsuit. I was struck by a wave of emotions: anger that it has taken this long to potentially see justice; concern that this is not enough, that there might be hidden conditions and agendas; heartache for the empty promises made by so many ministers and politicians, all attempting to appease the situation, with few of them ever acting on their words. It could have all had a greater positive outcome if only those in positions of power had applied their due diligence.

For fifteen year I tried to make safe drinking water a reality—I supported my late ex-husband, Dr. Hans Peterson, when he founded the Safe Drinking Water Foundation (SDWF) in 1996, and through our work with the foundation, we learned about the plight of Indigenous people in Canada, as well as folks who live in rural areas, and the struggle to ensure safe drinking water. Today, almost thirty years after we founded the SDWF, too many First Nations communities still don't have consistent access to this basic human right.

In a July 2021 article, *Water Canada* reports on the "long-awaited results" of Aboriginal Affairs and Northern Development Canada's study, titled the "National Assessment of Water and Wastewater Systems in First Nations Communities." Member of parliament Dr. Carolyn Bennett claims that the study "underscores the government's continued neglect, with nearly 1,800 First Nation community homes without water or sewage service, and $1.2 billion required immediately to bring these systems up to Aboriginal Affairs and Northern Development Canada's own protocol." She added that the problem is far more serious than previously reported, with 39 percent of First Nations drinking water systems rated as high risk by the assessment. The government has an obligation to commit additional new funding to address the immediate needs, in addition to an estimated $4.7 billion over the next 10 years.[3]

But the situation is not "far more serious than previously reported." It is as despicable as it has been reported—by the SDWF, among many others—for the past twenty-five years. Furthermore, if government had awarded contracts with a required means of measuring the quality of drinking water resulting from those contracts, then the money spent already, which far exceeds the planned billions to address the issue now, would not be necessary. The only difference is that someone is finally listening, or at least paying lip service to the issue.

Indeed, Nishnawbe Aski Nation (NAN) Deputy Grand Chief Terry Waboose said the study "merely confirms what NAN and First Nations across Canada have been telling the federal government for years—that there is a critical lack of infrastructure in First Nations communities. We don't need more studies to confirm what we have been saying for years."[4] These reports and assessments are only money in the coffers of colonial society and collect dust on bookshelves in the academy. It's long overdue for Canadian governments and engineering companies to step up and improve First Nations drinking water with guaranteed effective water treatment systems. Rural Canadians could benefit from the same support.

The national class action lawsuit was initiated in 2019 by the Neskantaga First Nation, Curve Lake First Nation and Tataskweyak Cree Nation and law firms Olthuis Kleer Townshend and McCarthy Tétrault. I am very pleased to see that Stephanie Willsey, an Indigenous lawyer, has been recognized for her contribution on this legal team.[5] The $8 billion settlement, called the First Nations Drinking Water Settlement, was agreed by the courts in December 2021, and includes compensation to individuals and affected First Nations, funds to "eligible individuals who suffered specified injuries due to a drinking water advisory that lasted at least one year between November 20, 1995, and June 20, 2021,... support for First Nations to develop their own safe drinking water bylaws and initiatives," and much more.[6]

While attention to these issues gives me some hope, I still have doubts that the best interests of these communities are the driving force behind these actions. Specifically, I find this statement problematic: compensation will be awarded to "eligible individuals who suffered specific injuries due to a drinking water advisory that lasted one year." I wonder how doctors are going to verify that anyone's illness was caused by unsafe drinking water. What about stillbirths or miscarriages? The skin rashes may be a little easier to verify. For years, I saw how water-borne illnesses were present far more often in First Nations and rural communities than in cities. Maybe a better way to assess those entitled to this compensation would be to test all possible source waters, thereby defining exactly what kind of process is required for effective treatment while also identifying those who have been exposed to water-borne illness.

Or, perhaps individuals should receive compensation based on how long they lived with a BWA. The use of the phrase "drinking water advisory" is additionally problematic; it's easy to downplay the severity of what a "boil water advisory" really means. Imagine boiling every drop of water you consume, whether to brush your teeth, wash your face or cook. Imagine trying to bathe babies, toddlers or young children while ensuring they don't take little mouthfuls of bath water. Imagine cleaning your fridge or stove with contaminated water. The Neskantaga First Nation community, with a population of four hundred people, has been under a BWA since 1995, twenty-eight years at this time of writing.

Dr. Nadine Burke Harris's research has proved the correlation between childhood adversity and illness later in life, be it heart attacks, asthma or strokes. Childhood trauma literally gets under our skin.[7] When families have endured living with unsafe water, they have experienced both physical and mental assaults on their bodies.

I would go so far as to say that politicians' neglect of the water crises in Indigenous communities for decades may have been as debilitating and atrocious as the residential schools. And it is still going on today.

With the six billion dollars set aside in the settlement for water treatment systems, all First Nations communities should have systems that meet or exceed the World Health Organization (WHO) regulations. Allowing Indigenous communities to "develop their own safe drinking water bylaws and initiatives" is the best scenario, and I foresee that with support and scientific knowledge they will lead Canada to drinking water regulations. Indigenous leaders should have the authority to decide which treatment processes they want for their communities. And it should not have taken this long.

Finally, and perhaps most problematically, anyone who accepts and participates in this claim process forgoes the opportunity for any future claims. But they still don't have safe drinking water, and Canada still doesn't have drinking water regulations. It is not enough, as Bennett claims in the *Water Canada* article, to have drinking water meet "Aboriginal Affairs and Northern Development Canada's own protocol." As Hans and I have argued from the beginning, Canada needs national drinking water *regulations*, meaning that violations against these regulations can be upheld by law. Guidelines, on the other hand, merely provide a goal to be strived for with no binding legal power. Guidelines have even less substance than standards, which set acceptable levels for certain compounds that can be found in the water; but meeting these standards may still not provide safe drinking water. Therefore, standards remain as little more than a formal set of guidelines.[8] I hope that this settlement is a step toward ensuring there are safe drinking water regulations in Canada, at least for First Nations. I predict that rural communities will soon follow the example of those involved in this lawsuit.

Through the SDWF, Hans and I spent fifteen years working to educate politicians about how to provide safe drinking water to all Indigenous and remote communities. In that time, I found myself in the middle of a national battle, married to the "mad scientist," as his son would affectionally call him, who tried his best to blow the whistle.

For me, it all started on the disco floor in Winnipeg, 1981.

1

The Swede with a PhD

It was Midsummer, June 21, 1981, and my co-workers helped me plan an evening out. They were going to Brandi's, the disco in downtown Winnipeg. They arranged for me to go with them that evening, and to take my babysitter home for me afterwards. I was thrilled to finally enjoy an evening out. I wasn't yet thirty years old, yet I felt I had aged way beyond my years. I was still reeling from my abusive marriage to P., whom I had separated from two years before. At the time, I couldn't enjoy a social life without the caring and planning of my dear friends. I had splurged on a new dress for the occasion, a sparkly red number. Rarely did I get to enjoy such a luxury; I had found it on a sales rack.

We stood in line for Brandi's and then, once inside, we waited for a table. Becoming impatient, my friend asked a young man sitting alone if he would share his table with us. That young man was named Hans Peterson.

Hans wore a crisp, cotton, light-coloured, short-sleeved shirt with epaulets on the shoulders, and he had a thick moustache. He looked and dressed European, and he had a face like an angelic cherub. As my friends got up to dance, Hans and I talked and talked. Hans's first wife had come with him to Winnipeg but had returned to Sweden. Midsummer was a big celebration in Sweden, and he was homesick.

Hans had all the education I'd ever dreamed of, and more besides. He knew everything, and about everything. I had left school at fifteen, a young woman in the suburbs of London in a hurry to leave home. I felt I knew nothing, or at least nothing about anything he discussed. Acid rain? I had no idea what it was, and I didn't know what pipettes were when he started talking about his collection. But we shared an interest in leftist politics. We were both anti-racism, anti-establishment, anti-arms and anti-war. He had been rejected from compulsory military service in Sweden because he would not fire a weapon if his life depended upon it. He reiterated my own thoughts and beliefs. British military had come to my secondary school more than once to recruit. Friends who attended the higher level of education in public grammar schools have reaffirmed to me that the military never attempted to recruit from those schools. I figured they thought that folks from council estates who attended the secondary schools were cheap fodder for war. And I was against war. I was all about "make love and not war." I was a genuine hippie from London.

I felt that Hans and I were two compassionate and caring people. We were convinced that we could make the world a better place. I was totally enamored, besotted maybe, that anyone with a PhD would look twice at me, never mind talk to me. He had me at our first discussion.

Eventually, we made it to the busy dance floor, packed by Winnipeg standards. Hands and arms were held high, swaying in the air, waving in sync with each other, *Y-M-C-A*. Hans could not keep the beat to any song, but it was the era of doing your own thing on the dance floor and it went unnoticed. I didn't mind at all. A slow dance wrapped up the evening and, before we went our separate ways, Hans asked me for my phone number.

⚔

This new, interesting man was a welcome distraction from my life. In June of 1970, I had emigrated from Liverpool aboard the steamship RMS *Empress of Canada*, which heaved into the Saint Lawrence River after a rocky transatlantic crossing. P., my husband, and I had arrived in the city of Montreal. I was a possession listed on his passport, my only qualification a high school diploma, and all our belongings were packed into two suitcases. I was eighteen years old. P. and I then took the train from Montreal to Winnipeg.

Everyone I met in Winnipeg was smitten with my London accent. I met other Brits; many of them were teachers or nurses. They were from the more affluent areas of London, and I quickly became acutely aware that my accent gave away the poor area of London where I grew up. When I spoke, I often said "me" when I should have said "my" or "I." My grammar left a lot to be desired, but Canadians thought it cute. At every opportunity, I tried to learn the proper grammar, but my accent stayed with me.

I soon realized that P. appeared to be allergic to work and loved to party. I switched jobs a couple of times, often working a daytime job in addition to a part-time evening or weekend job. When I was hired at Eaton's, the minimum wage was $1.35 per hour and soon increased to $1.50. What I had earned in a week in England I earned in a day at Eaton's.

I slowly worked my way up. Working at Eaton's was like being part of a huge family. Four years after my emigration, I was promoted to Buyer for women's designer fashions. I had to fly to Toronto for my first buying trip and I was terrified, as I had never flown before. Afterwards, I travelled to Los Angeles, New York, Las Vegas, as well as more frequently to Montreal and Toronto, where I bought lines like Anne Klein. In New York, I met Calvin Klein when he launched his signature tight-fitting jeans that established him in the Canadian market. He was a smooth playboy with a tremendous amount of money behind him and an ego to match.

As a buyer, I felt a huge responsibility and always asked about the rights of the workers. How many hours a week are they working? Do they have benefits? What about sick leave? Coffee and lunch breaks? Management always assured me that my concerns were unfounded, making me feel as though they thought it inappropriate for me to ask such questions. I often asked to tour the factory floor. I recall the sea of black hair of predominantly Filipino women, bent over their sewing machines, intent on maintaining their hourly quota, their feet and hands working in unison. Occasionally, a woman would lift her head, just for a second, and our eyes would connect. In those flash encounters between women, a woman laid bare her soul. I felt the reassurances were lies. I thought about their challenges, their despair, their need to feed their families. What could I do? I carried their despair knowing I couldn't do any more than keep pushing and asking. At the end of the day, I was powerless. Meanwhile, the rich customers were shopping with their friends, trying to impress each other with how much money they spent for an outfit for whatever happened to be the next "who's who" event in their social network, or buying their mistresses expensive gifts.

In 1976, I was offered the position of sales manager at the Garden City Store, which was the closest location to St. Andrew's, where I was living with P. at the time. It was a perfect fit for me. I was in my element; I came to Canada to fulfill my dream to better myself and I couldn't have wished for anything to be more perfect. I was moving up the ladder of success. I loved my work, and I loved the people I worked with. I got to travel and meet new people and I had a great bunch of friends. I didn't recognize P.'s abusive behaviour for what it was, but then I had no idea domestic abuse existed. Then I became pregnant.

On January 15, 1976, Adam was born. At that time, mothers were allowed a maximum of six weeks maternity leave. Once my maternity leave was over, at work every three hours, or as it coincided with my breaks, I sat on a toilet seat in the lady's washroom and hand-pumped my milk to store with an icepack in a cooler, hidden in the stockroom. Each night, I took it home and filled bottles for Adam's feedings the following day. My heart was torn into a million pieces. I would have loved to stay home and raise my son, but since P. had lost his job, I was the sole breadwinner and I had no choice. If I thought our marriage was bad before Adam was born, it was nothing compared to what life was like after my second son, Mark, was born.

I don't know how I found the strength to go to a lawyer, but one day I did. I will always appreciate the lawyer's foresight and advice. He not only arranged for a court date the next morning for me, but he also made phone calls on my behalf, he arranged for an apartment close to my work and preschool and for a moving company to move my things. I was so terribly fragile and barely functioning, and he recognized that.

This was my situation when Hans entered our lives: I was a single mum, working full-time with my two precious young boys in daycare, renting a small apartment where the Formica countertops were peeling and the walls were so thin, but the apartment was a godsend all the same. Adam and Mark loved to play together in the kitchen cupboards, climbing and crawling inside them for hours. I had nothing else to put in the cupboards. I finalized my divorce with P. a year later.

In the beginning, Hans took our complicated situation in stride. There were ongoing challenges with counselling for Adam and Mark, and I had difficulty communicating with my ex-husband. I was traumatized: if a motorbike or car backfired outside, the blood drained from my face and I shook from head to toe, deathly afraid that my ex was outside with a gun. But Hans was a calming influence, and we needed calming. He had called me the morning after Brandi's, suggesting he cook me dinner. He cooked a great filet steak. More than anything, we enjoyed great conversations. Hans didn't seem at all bothered that I had two young sons and that it was challenging for me to find a babysitter for our dates. He quickly offered to do things together, like day trips to lakes and impromptu barbeques. He enjoyed playing with the boys, kicking a soccer ball around, and he quickly stepped up to look after them when I worked evenings or weekends. He became a great father figure. I was besotted, and I struggled to accept that he liked me. Soon, Hans, Mark, Adam and I fell into a simple routine as a happy family.

Hans was eccentric. It was obvious to everyone who met him. He had, for example, bought an old second-hand bike that he painted bright red. He rode it everywhere, never needing to lock it as no one else would have wanted to ride such a bike.

I had a cousin who had earned his doctorate back in the UK, and other than him, I did not know anyone who had been to univer-

sity, let alone for nine years to
earn a PhD. Hans loved to talk
about his research on acid rain,
but I had never heard the words
in his vocabulary before. He
would patiently explain to me
what he was working on, like
the damage to nature through
the acidification of soils, lakes
and seas, and when I would ask
what acidification meant, he
would launch into details of pH
levels. I would ask what "pH
levels" meant, and on and on it
would go. The bottom line was
that I was flattered that anyone
so educated would be interested in me, someone who had left
school at fifteen. And I liked
eccentric. I liked anyone who
stood up against the status quo.

Hans rode his bright red, second-hand
bike everywhere.

In the summer of 1982, we drove to Vancouver Island. Hans
had job interviews with the Department of Fisheries and Oceans in
Sidney and Nanaimo, and I was eager for him to accept one of the
positions. I loved the idea of living beside the sea, and the milder
winters were a big attraction for me. We spent a week with friends
in Sidney and drove to Nanaimo for the day, but it wasn't meant to
be. Hans declared he hated it on the island: "There is nothing to do
here, the water is too cold to swim in, and you can't cycle because
there are too many hills. As for hiking in the mountains, they just
aren't exciting trails," he claimed. So, we continued living in Winnipeg and Hans continued his work at the Freshwater Institute.

Instead, we found an old house in Winnipeg we could reno-
vate, and we qualified for a new government program for homebuy-
ers. Mortgage rates were at a record high of 18 percent! I am not

sure where I left my head when we decided to take on this daunting project. Slowly, we renovated that old house and transformed it into our home. It was very important to Hans that our home have a Swedish design. I loved that style, too, so I found it easy to decorate with a Scandinavian flair. The pine ceiling, the maple flooring and our pine furniture all contributed to our Scandinavian home.

The back garden had a lane at the rear where a huge, old oak tree provided the boys with the best possible play structure. I turned the entire backyard into a vegetable garden and managed to grow an abundance of veggies, enough to freeze and feed us for the entire winter. I'm not sure how we accomplished all we did with the state of that house. I remember making lunches on makeshift orange boxes as we had no kitchen cupboards, and brushing sawdust out of the boys' hair before sending them off to school.

I had tremendous energy then, matched only by my passion for life. These combined traits meant I took on way too many projects. From when Adam was first born, I always spent my time playing with the children when they were awake. Once they settled in bed, I began to do things like laundry, cleaning and preparing the next day's meals. I don't think I ever went to bed before midnight, and the alarm clock always rang too early at 5:30 a.m.

I loved my job at Eaton's. I had been promoted to Soft Goods Inventory Control Manager for Western Canada, yet more important than the title and the pay was the fact that I now worked from eight a.m. to four p.m., Monday to Friday. Although I was in heaven, no longer required to work evenings and weekends, upper management decided that I needed to learn computer programming. So, I attended Red River College two nights a week, where I tried to learn FORTRAN and COBOL. I failed miserably at my new languages, but attending the classes kept management happy and I quickly learned that common sense was going to prevail: I didn't need to learn how to program a computer to use it effectively. A room about 2,500 square feet was built to house the computer. Although the room was twice the size of most houses, the computer barely fit in it. I worked with a great team of about twenty women.

I continued to be the main breadwinner, as we did not know when Hans might get paid for a contract. "I'm scrambling," he would exclaim repeatedly, as if it was an excuse for being late meeting deadlines.

2

Early Married Life

Hans and I were married on December 30, 1983. There were nine of us at the Justice of the Peace office on Provencher: my girlfriend and her husband, my parents, my brother, and Mark and Adam.

Adam had been moved into grade one without completing kindergarten and Mark was in kindergarten. Maybe it was my love of reading and how often I read with them that encouraged their reading abilities, but they both read well before they attended school. Mark was also dyslexic. I worked with him daily to overcome his struggles. It reached the point where he would ask me, "Do I have to write it your way or can I write it my way?" He could switch from writing normal to writing in absolute mirror fashion in the blink of an eye.

Mark was not impressed with his teacher. He wanted her recognition and praise, but he didn't get it. One day, he came home from school and announced, "Well, she knows I can read and write now."

"How does she know?" I asked.

"Because I wrote in big letters on the chalkboard, 'The Mad Scientist,' and I told her that's my dad!" Mark was glowing with pride, proud of his dad, proud of his spelling. Hans certainly lived up to his description as the Mad Scientist as the years progressed.

Hans, being full of ideas, was convinced that Swedish giftware would be very popular in Canada. I loved Swedish design and culture and needed no persuading. I typed hundreds of letters on an Olivetti manual typewriter to Swedish or Scandinavian companies exploring the possibility of selling their products in Canada. I was amazed that so many of those I approached were happy to be introduced to the Canadian market. I thought, perhaps naïvely, that this new venture would allow for me to earn money while spending more time with my children. In hindsight, I had drastically underestimated the time and dedication required to build a business from scratch.

While preparing to explore my new career, I became pregnant, and Sven was born March 10, 1985. Hans was beside himself with anxiety, and the fact that Sven was a breach birth made it even harder for both of us. (Although I am sure it was hardest for me, Hans would have disagreed.)

Sven was an extremely colicky baby, yet he was so quiet and calm considering the discomfort he was going through. I walked the floor at night for hours, his head resting on my shoulder, patting his back. If I stopped, he cried. As Sven grew older, he would always pat my back in return. When he was comfortable, Sven would sit contentedly for the longest periods of time. Asta, Hans's mother, said he reminded her of Hans, who she said always sat like a lit candle.

Hans couldn't take time at night to help. He explained, "I need my sleep to function. My work is important and intellectual." I don't recall his reason why he was not able to change diapers. There was no doubt that he loved his son, but he showed it in his own unique way. This wasn't unusual for the times: few men stepped up to help with running the home or parenting the children, so I didn't think anything of it. I was happy, and I worshipped Hans and his work. Wasn't that what a good wife was supposed to do? It never occurred to me to think otherwise.

We began to merge our family traditions, and Christmas became a huge celebration. Hans was involved in preparing many traditional Swedish dishes. The highlight of Christmas soon became the visit of Santa in person each Christmas Eve, as was the Swedish tradition. It was fun to get Hans dressed up, and it was never difficult to convince the children he had to go back to work while we prepared him as Santa Claus. I think Hans most enjoyed drinking the aquavit as he was dressing up.

The giftware business I had started, Petersons' Scandinavian Products, was progressing nicely, although not as planned: instead, I was hosting home parties and my dear friends had given me a great start. Then, friends of friends attending the parties began hosting and I was often working three or four evenings, or some weekend afternoons, selling the Scandinavian giftware and furniture. I was pregnant once again; each time I was pregnant, I felt so energized, healthy and happy, and I took on way more than I should have. I had hosted a home party on June 27 and was standing in line at the bank to deposit the money the next morning when my water broke, and I went into labour with Elsa.

She was another breach birth, and I was furious with the attending doctor, who said, "You've done this before; you can do it again." I was furious with Hans, too, for not advocating for me to have a caesarian birth. All the same, Elsa Jane was born on June 28, 1986, and I was so happy to name her after my Nana, Elsie Margaret Jane. I was high in the clouds with happiness. I had my perfect family.

Once we were home from the hospital, life was stressful, and Hans couldn't take any time off work from the Freshwater Institute to help me. Our home was in turmoil with renovations on hold, but at least we had kitchen cupboards, after almost three years without. I needed to step right back into doing everything a mother does for a family. With my newborn, Sven, fourteen months old, Mark seven and Adam ten, I had my hands full. Adam stepped up and became a great help to me. He and Mark were super big brothers. Elsa was so easy to care for, always smiling. Her huge, dark brown eyes were identical to Mark's, and with her long lashes, her looks pierced everyone's heart. She was vocal and fiercely independent, always pushing to do more ahead of her age. Her brothers nicknamed her Miss Push.

When Hans was home from work in time, he was fabulous at telling bedtime stories to the children. He always personalized each story, adding an old man and a little boy named Sven or Mark or Adam. The children loved his stories. I was sad that he was rarely home to put them to bed. But he woke the children up each morning singing a song, which became a lovely routine for us each and every day.

I enjoyed four months of maternity leave. For a couple of weeks, I took Elsa with me to open a showroom in Richmond Hill near Toronto for my business, now incorporated and named Svensk Corp. I also took Elsa with me to New York where I presented my wares at a trade show held at the prestigious Javits Center. I tried hard to make my new business profitable so that I could quit Eaton's and work from home to be with my children. While I thoroughly enjoyed my work, creating my own business, I would have loved to stay home with my children. It was a huge mistake on my part. How I wish now that I had simply settled for less and been content to enjoy every little progress they achieved. We still could not rely on any income from Hans, so after my maternity leave was over, I reluctantly returned to work at Eaton's.

Sometimes, the overwhelming amount of work made me feel as though the days would never end, but more often I fell into bed never wanting my life to change or the children to grow up. I loved every day with my perfect family, and I coined a phrase that I would repeat over the next decade or more: "I wish I could freeze this day to last forever."

In January 1987, Hans was headhunted and asked to attend an interview with the Saskatchewan Research Council (SRC) in Saskatoon. When Hans completed the interview they offered him the position, but he didn't call me to tell me the good news. Instead, he called our friends, who had commented a couple of weeks previously that if we moved, they wanted to buy our house. Hans made an agreement with them that they would buy our house and move into it in a month's time. Then, he called me to share the news: he had accepted the position for March 15, he had sold our house and we would need to move by March 1.

I was sad to leave my work at Eaton's, and I would miss my

Hans in his laboratory at the Freshwater Institute in Winnipeg.

many friends. There were no openings for me to transfer to Eaton's in Saskatoon, so we decided that I should take this opportunity to work solely on Svensk Corp. It would be a significant pay cut for me, and I was nervous about the change, as Hans's SRC wage was less than what I earned at Eaton's.

As we prepared to move, Hans and I had been together for six years and married for four. We left Winnipeg excited about our new adventure in Saskatoon. Hans drove with the boys while Elsa and I flew, as the only car we owned, a Mazda 626, only had five seats.

I held mixed emotions as we embarked on this new life, exploring the unknown, a repeat of my immigration to Canada in 1970. But I also held emotions of hope, of relief, that maybe now I wouldn't have to work so hard. I dreamed of enjoying more time with my children.

3

Moving to the Farm

There were few houses for sale with immediate possession dates when we were house hunting in Saskatoon. We picked a brick, two-storey home with a fenced yard, an attached garage (a huge luxury) and a typical front lawn on a quiet side road, easy for the children to walk to schools through Lakeview Park. It was a huge step up from our Winnipeg neighbourhood and home.

We had brought *The Pig*, our heavy canoe, with us from Winnipeg, and Hans made sure canoeing became our favourite pastime each summer. We felt the South Saskatchewan River was Saskatoon's best-kept secret. It wasn't long before we were not all able to fit in one canoe and we bought *Snow White* and then *Sunshine* clipper canoes, named for their colours. I would often paddle with Adam and Mark, and Hans would paddle a canoe single-handed with Sven and Elsa. We enjoyed many blissful canoe trips, paddling along, listening to nature, happy kids singing their favourite songs—"I like peanut butter"... "the cat came back"—nothing mattered when we were out on the water; life was perfect.

Hans had begun a project called "Algae in Dugouts" with the SRC, and it was through this project that he first encountered poor water quality in Canada. "I couldn't believe that people would drink such murky-looking water and without in-house treatment to boot," Hans says in a Rural Councillor article from 1997. He formed a Water Quality section within the SRC that was committed to raising awareness of drinking water quality and providing solutions, both nationally and internationally.[9]

Through this early research with the SRC, Hans was beginning to understand why rural communities in Canada had such poor water quality and why their water treatment systems are largely neglected by government agencies. City dwellers, by contrast, often get their water through non-contaminated and non-challenging watersheds like the Rocky Mountains, from which many cities across Western Canada get their water. And because contaminated water is one of the most efficient ways to spread disease since the water can reach everyone on the piped water supply within hours, scientists and engineers evaluate the water source daily, sometimes hourly, in cities. These two factors often protect city water from disease-causing microbes, which can be contained in particles that are difficult to break down or kill with chlorine.[10] Rural communities, on the other hand, often source water from rain and snow collections in agricultural fields, which feed small reservoirs and shallow wells. The quality of this water is typically poor. As Hans writes,

> not only is this water much more difficult to treat, but in addition, the research and development carried out by most cities to provide safe drinking water simply does not exist for rural water supplies. To make matters worse, when the provinces get together with federal agencies to discuss the Canadian Drinking Water Quality Guidelines (about every six months), rural drinking water has never reached the table. These guidelines were designed to protect city dwellers. ... If the efforts carried out by cities were to be matched for rural Canada, research and development laboratories with several hundred people would be required to solve the much tougher and diverse quality problems affecting rural areas. Small communities and individual rural water users are generally using inadequate treatment equipment to deal with these large challenges.[11]

"The end result," Hans concludes, "has been to leave rural people with the poorest water in Canada and few options to deal with it."[12]

I continued to worship Hans and his important scientific work as we settled into our life in Saskatoon. I never gave a thought to him prioritizing his work above our family. As he eased into his role, I found a small warehouse for Svensk Corp. Gradually, doors opened in paper party products, and I saw an opportunity to market my products to grocery chains. I began designing serviettes and paper party products made from recycled paper, which proved to be successful across Canada. It was the beginning of the era of the three Rs—reduce, reuse, recycle—and timing proved profitable.

An Alberta company represented my products in Western Canada, and they had links to US grocery stores. Soon my products were in Washington and Oregon. One day, I had a phone call with a buyer from a US grocery chain.

"We supply display racks to stand freely in your store," I said to him, providing him with my regular sales pitch. "On it, we merchandise recycled paper party products, tablecloths, napkins, coasters, candles and candle rings, all colour coordinated for the season."

"Colour-coordinated napkins?" he repeated questioningly.

"Yes, colour-coordinated napkins to go with the tablecloths and candles. We have different themes for Thanksgiving, Valentines, all the holidays."

The buyer was quite flabbergasted. He kept asking me to repeat what I had said. "Colour-coordinated napkins?" Reluctantly, he bought into our program. It was a month or so later when I realized that in Europe, everyone refers to *serviettes* as *napkins*. I had carried that description to my marketing. In Canada, *napkins* are referred to as *serviettes*—but in America, *napkins* are actually *sanitary* pads! The poor man thought hostesses were colour coordinating their sanitary pads to their dinner parties. And he bought into it!

Hans was very good at securing contracts for which we—the children and I, that is—had to do a lot of the manual labour. One such contract was to put hundreds of ducks on all the storm water retention ponds in Regina. Hans monitored the water quality during the summer and the objective was to reduce the algae and the number of mosquitos, which he successfully accomplished. At the end of summer we then had to catch the ducks; their wings had been clipped so they could not fly away so they were unable to migrate, and they could not remain on the small bodies of water for the six months of winter. Catching them became a skill in itself. We took two or more canoes out into the lake and, with a length of orange snow fence strung between canoes, we herded the ducks toward a specific area, where we tried to channel them to folks waiting to catch them and put them in cages. Rarely did we manage this roundup without at least one canoe capsizing. I made sure the ducks all went to the soup kitchens, so the homeless people ate well that week. We were exhausted at the end of each roundup.

One day, Hans came home with a large aquarium and a bucket of baby tilapia fish. He had a contract to research the potential damage to other fish caused by the tilapia if the fish were released

The children and me catching ducks on a storm water retention pond in Regina.

into the wild. Hans set up an enormous aquarium in the basement of our house in Saskatoon. This became the hub of entertainment and learning for our kids and all their friends.

I was shocked at how rapidly the tilapia grew. In no time, it seemed they began jumping out of the aquarium, flip flopping and splashing around on our hardwood floor. They made such a commotion that we heard them from upstairs, and someone would quickly run down to place them back in the tank. No matter how we tried to block them from escaping, the bigger they grew, the stronger they were to jump out.

One night, I put the children to bed and then joined Hans and his parents, Asta and Gosta in the living room. The conversation moved to how much Sven resembled his dad, and in so many ways. The next morning, Elsa came down for breakfast and I couldn't believe my eyes: she had cut the front of her hair, close to her forehead, not just her bangs but all her hair from the top of her head. I asked her why, to which she replied, "I want to be like Daddy too." I had no idea she had been listening to our conversation the previous evening.

Shortly after, we took Asta and Gosta canoeing down the South Saskatchewan River. We came across an older couple living in a lovely old home on the riverbank in the rural municipality of Rudy, otherwise known as Outlook. They made us very welcome, proud to share the bounty of their garden with us, and they encouraged us to explore land for sale adjacent to their property. We were able to purchase the land, just over fifty acres, a short time later. There was much work to be done before we could move to the property, including building a home to live in. We immediately started dreaming and planning. The top priority was to dig trenches for the tilapia fish.

Shortly after we purchased the farmland, we bought an old mobile home that we moved to the property, and a year later we added a second mobile home. We renovated them to make one large home, aligned somewhat like a letter V or L, and we moved to the farm that summer. I have always loved architecture and design, and

Hans and his buddies, Tom, Nick and Howard.

I was in my element designing how our new home would look and how the two mobile homes could be constructed together. We had many skylights and windows; in summer, it was a beautiful home, with no blinds or curtains. We felt like we lived outdoors. I disconnected the television, and we went six years without it. I planted a robust vegetable garden.

Meanwhile, as sales of Svensk Corp's paper party products proved successful for grocery stores, one grocery chain demanded that I also make displays in French for them to market in Quebec. Selling in this province was completely new territory for me and entailed a business strategy I had not anticipated nor budgeted for. Eventually, this expansion resulted in such a huge loss to me that I was not able to stay in business. Reluctantly, I sold part of the business for Western grocery stores to the sales company that represented my line in Western Canada. I closed my business to Eastern Canada and my warehouse in Saskatoon for good.

In 1992, I was very happy to be hired by the Saskatchewan Abilities Council as the communications manager for the province of Saskatchewan. Fundraising was my number one responsibility. This was a role that was totally in line with my values and my heart.

At home during this time, rarely were there less than ten at the dinner table. Hans had three close scientist buddies, Tom, Nick and Howard, all scientists from his university days in Dundee. They enjoyed collaborating on their science projects and often prepared applications for grants with the objective of further collaboration. Hans also supervised PhD students, who often worked in foreign countries but came annually for a short time to work in Hans's lab with him. When they visited, they often stayed with us the first few nights while I showed them around Saskatoon and made sure they were set up independently in the city. I thoroughly enjoyed each visitor. I loved having company, cooking and being a gracious hostess. I wouldn't change any of those times, but I sure was exhausted.

As if life wasn't hectic enough, I decided we should have a puppy join our family. An ad in the local paper offered Old English Sheepdog puppies, a breed I had fond memories of from my childhood in the UK. We went to see the puppies at a farm outside Saskatoon, and we did what every family does when they go to see puppies: we came home with one. Mark named her Odin, "Because Odin is the God of all Gods and God is DOG spelled backwards, and she is the Dog of all Dogs," he exclaimed. And so, Odin became a much-loved member of our family.

Hans and his university buddy Nick built long trenches to grow the tilapia outside. Hans also designed a water treatment system for the property. It was based on a huge, lined dugout, constructed like an inverted pyramid. Water was pumped through a trench from the South Saskatchewan River, held in the dugout before moving through various filtration membranes and then finally piped to our home. The plan was to pump water from the river to fill the dugout as required.

We had only lived at the farm for a month or two when we took a road trip back to Winnipeg. On our homeward journey, Hans read scientific papers, as he always did while I drove. On this journey, he also enjoyed bags of wine gums and red liquorice, two of his favourite candies. We were approaching the town of Davidson when he began to appear ill. He looked extremely tired, and he said he had

Odin, the "Dog of all Dogs."

blurred vision and headache. I wasn't very sympathetic, blaming his diet, but I soon decided that we should stop at the Davidson hospital, as it would be another hour until we got home.

Within minutes of entering the hospital, the nurses had him in a bed and hooked up to an intravenous drip. The doctor announced that he would not be going home that night; he had acute type 2 diabetes and needed medication. Hans never wavered throughout his life: he refused to take medication and was adamant he could treat his diabetes with exercise and diet.

Around this time, Hans became obsessed with self-sustained living. I bought into the romantic notion of it all, having always tried to grow as much of my own food as possible wherever I had lived. I was always a flower child at heart, and I loved the idea of children playing in nature and of living off the earth. However, the one-hour drive each way to the city, on a highway with no shoulders and lots of potholes, quickly took its toll. My long workdays were too much. Plus, the children were missing out on various sports activities, having to also travel over an hour each way on the school bus to

Outlook school. The farm animals, the sheer amount of work and the bills we were incurring gave me a persistent sick feeling in the pit of my stomach. I wanted desperately to renege on all we had taken on. Hans refused. I was shattering our dream.

Something else was also happening. I was, for the most part, a single mum all over again, as Hans was away from home for more time each year. He was travelling for work, visiting his foreign PhD students or collaborating with scientists and attending conferences around the world. I stood behind him and his work, but I was beginning to feel in over my head.

The trench we built from the South Saskatchewan river to bring water to our home.

4

Freezing Over, Heating Up

One day, the children had been playing in the nearby forest metres from our house when, fifteen minutes later, we lost two bred cows to a cougar attack. I had to figure out how we could safely continue to let our children run free exploring the countryside. A conservation officer advised us that the best protection from cougars was to get dogs that would stay with the children. So, I began looking for another Old English Sheepdog to join Odin. I had a hard time finding puppies, but I eventually found Freya and Loki. Sensing a business opportunity, I thought we should get an unrelated male so we could breed them. Within the next year or so, I bought more puppies. Bragi, Saga and Hlin were next to join Freya and Loki. We kept the tradition of Norse mythology that Mark had initiated when he named Odin—who refused to ever be bred and remained an old maid. So began my Old English Sheepdog breeding program.

The first winter at the farm crept up on us. We had grossly underestimated the cold, the winds and the challenges to keep warm. Life on the Prairies in the winter was all about survival. We quickly learned that pumping water when it was -40° Celsius was next to impossible. A huge problem developed as vermin drowned in the dugout, and as ice formed a solid, deep layer over the surface, lack of oxygen was another huge factor. I became disillusioned: that winter, we first encountered foul-smelling water, then extreme water rationing.

After lots of complaining by me, Hans eventually improved the filtration system in what we named the Pump House, built under the

An aerial view of our farm located in the rural municipality of Rudy on the banks of the South Saskatchewan River.

garage in a vertical culvert. We had reverse osmosis systems at all sinks in the house to protect us, but they were high maintenance. Hans always intended to further tweak our system, but he never got around to it. The cobbler's children go barefoot, as the saying goes. Mice seemed to occupy every possible cupboard where plumbing provided the slightest opportunity to enter and escape the cold. Five months of winter seemed to last twenty years.

What I hated most about the Pump House was that it was an upturned culvert, placed on its end, approximately three metres high. A stepladder was directly below the trap door. To enter, I had to hold my body over the trap door, holding my body weight on my elbows, dropping my feet first, dangling them, hoping to find the top of the stepladder with my toes to balance, then climb down to the dank, salamander-infested concrete floor. I always had my heart in my mouth as I descended, wondering whether, if I slipped, I would die a quick death or a slow, painful one, as it might take the kids a while to figure out where I was. When I shared my worries with my neighbour, she insisted I call her whenever I went down there and again when I returned safely, or they would come looking for me.

I desperately wanted to return to the city, but Hans was un-yielding. He wanted cattle, a milk cow, chickens, sheep, you name it. He bought old, worn-out cowboy boots from the neighbouring farmer and a cowboy hat from Agribition. He became obsessed with living the life of a cowboy. The end of the world was nigh, and for Hans, the self-sustaining lifestyle of the farm was the solution. He was adamant that his scientific expertise would enable us to be self-sufficient and that we had to prepare. He began stockpiling supplies at the farm.

As difficult as things were becoming between Hans and me, rarely did a day go by when I didn't treasure every minute with my children. *I wish I could freeze this day to last forever*. I loved every day together, whether it was tobogganing in the winter or canoeing or swimming in the river in the summer. I loved playing with them, shouting my support at various sports games (I especially loved soccer) and preparing their favourite meals for their birthdays. I was always happiest with my children around me.

Soon after we moved to the farm, Adam moved to live in the city. Farm life was not cool for a city teenager. A year or so later, Mark completed high school in Outlook, and with his fellow gradu-ates, we celebrated with a wonderful breakfast at the farm following a night of celebrating. He then joined a combine harvest crew and left for the States for the summer.

At the time, Hans was conducting research on diquat and Roundup. He visited many rural residents and farmers, and he was concerned about its adverse effects on humans and on aquatic life. In many ways, he was ahead of his time. He tried to alert people not to use talcum powder, especially on babies and young children, claiming it was carcinogenic. He also alerted the public to stop us-ing the hard blue sanitizers that were hung in diaper pails for the same reason. His research was alerting him to the fact that diquat might be carcinogenic too.

One weekend in the middle of summer, I flew to Toronto for a work conference. I hated being away longer than I had to; the airline's marketing ploy required passengers stay over a Saturday night to get lowest pricing, infringing on family time. So, I got up in the middle of the night to get the earliest flight back to Saskatoon on the Sunday morning. The contrast of Toronto, the city of concrete, the buzz of information I had gleaned from impressive speakers, compared to the farm where contentment and tranquility reigned, was huge. I loved being home.

I saddled up two horses, one for Sven and Elsa, and the other for me. We went for a ride in the open prairie. The view was spectacular: the river valley, the undulating native prairie where wild buffalo or moose had once roamed, sandbars with luxurious white sand and willow saplings whispering in the gentle breeze. We rode past the dip, a gulley where water ran to the river after a heavy rain, then back to open prairie. When we returned, I tied the two horses to the corral fence beside the barn and Elsa and Sven began helping me to remove their tack.

"Go to the other side of the fence to take off their bridles," I called to Sven and Elsa. "I don't like the way they are acting."

I had barely finished speaking when Bella reared up, startling the second horse, who also reared up. Both horses immediately became frantic, and as they panicked, they pulled the top fence rail to which their lead ropes were tethered. The rail lifted into the air and came crashing onto the back of my head. I hit the ground face first and was knocked unconscious. The horses thundered off across the pasture, the rail dragging behind them.

Hans had come running. I came to with Hans shaking me, saying, "I don't know what to do, Sue, don't pass out, I don't know what to do!"

"Stop fucking shaking me!" I replied and passed out again.

The next thing I remember, I was lying on the couch in the living room and Wanda—our neighbour and dear friend, who also happened to be an ICU nurse—was beside me. Everyone decided that I needed to get to a hospital. All I remember thinking was that I was so grateful Elsa and Sven hadn't been hurt.

I stayed at the Royal University Hospital in Saskatoon for two weeks. I had fractured my skull, a bloody mucous was draining from my right ear and I had a huge hematoma at the nape of my neck, so large I could not cover it entirely with the palm of my hand. I felt like I had grown a painful horn from the back of my neck. I had to sleep on my side, and still do today: although it eventually shrank back to normal, the spot where I had the hematoma still causes too much pain if I lie flat on the back of my head. I had also suffered a severe concussion and whiplash.

When I returned home, I could not tolerate any sunlight, and our beautiful, large windows and skylights let in so much light. I spent the next three months isolated in our bedroom with the blinds down. I felt like I was perpetually beneath a helicopter with its blades rapidly rotating, the pressure and noise bearing down on my head.

Hans claimed he had to live in Saskatoon to work long hours at the SRC. Our home in the city had sold, so he found a rooming house, where the other tenants were mostly taxi drivers, and he focussed all his time and efforts on his work. I felt isolated physically, socially, mentally and emotionally. Looking back, I think the isolation and loneliness were worse than the fractured skull, whiplash and concussion combined. All I could do was cry. And I cried a great deal.

After a few months of recuperation, I tried to return to work. I desperately wanted to return; I loved my job and everything it entailed. No matter how hard I tried, however, I could only handle a couple of hours until I could feel my face freezing, and my ability to complete mental tasks or even communicate and participate in discussions rapidly deteriorated. I asked for part-time hours to ease my return, but the Saskatchewan Abilities Council told me my role could only be done as a full-time employee. They shocked me with their next statement: they were letting me go because I was not available for full-time work. Their decision cut off the disability insurance I had been receiving; overnight, I had no more income. To me, this was disgustingly cruel. The Saskatchewan Abilities Council was an organization that catered to people with physical or mental disabilities, which sometimes resulted from brain injuries. I found their decision reflected their lack of empathy and understanding. I cried inconsolably.

A short time passed before I contacted the federal human rights organization, which accepted my case for review. It was little consolation; our financial worries were critical. I kept everything inside. Depression and anxiety controlled my every move, my every thought. My two young children were doing their best to take care of me.

※

By the summer of 1996, I was still struggling to live a normal life. I couldn't tolerate loud noise, especially conversation when people talked over each other or music, and bright lights still exasperated me. I was on the phone to the Human Rights Commission when they told me the good news of their ruling: after months of gathering information, almost a year after my accident, they ruled that I had been wrongfully dismissed by the Saskatchewan Abilities Council. I was overcome with emotion. Suddenly, I dropped the phone as I began vomiting uncontrollably. I lost control of my body and there was intense pain in my head. I knew I was seriously ill.

My parents were visiting the farm, and Sven and Elsa were also home. I was trying to speak to them, but I couldn't communicate or articulate my words. No one understood my garble. They helped me to our bedroom where I lay on top of the bed, sweating profusely, shaking uncontrollably. My mother kept refreshing cold cloths that she draped over my head while she ranted: "Damn stupid, you moving out here, living in the middle of nowhere. You need your brains tested!" I had so much to say and I was trying so hard to say it, but they had no idea what I was saying.

Hours went by. Miraculously, Adam came by the farm unexpectedly. He immediately took control of the situation, and they took me to the hospital. I had suffered a stroke. Regrettably, I arrived at the hospital six hours after the stroke's onset. I had a very long and challenging recovery ahead of me.

I lost the ability to process information, and I could not read or write. Because I lost some peripheral vision, the doctors pulled my driver's licence. My ophthalmologist told me that I had two permanent areas of lost vision that would never return. They were like icicles coming from the sky and penetrating 30 percent of my upper outer peripheral vision on both eyes. He told me, "You can see all buildings, all vehicles, all people, but what you won't see is if a plane drops out of the sky for an emergency landing on the highway ahead of you. You won't see it coming, and maybe that is a good thing." He laughed as he told me this, but when he said that I had a less than 10 percent chance of getting my licence back, I was devastated.

Elsa's encouragement gave me the push I needed. "Mum," she said, "every night on the weather they say it's a 10 percent chance of rain and it always rains, so it's okay. You'll get your licence back."

Doctors assured me that Premarin, a medication I was on, had no part in my stroke, and that it was a clot that broke away from my original head injury. I felt doctors were protecting doctors. In the USA, there is a class action lawsuit for all patients who had strokes after being prescribed Premarin when they had a family history of stroke. It does not apply to Canadians. This personal experience is why I doubt First Nations people will be able to have doctors' support in stating that any illness they suffered was due to their water.

I returned to the farm after a two-week stay at the hospital, and Hans accepted contracts to work in Thailand. We had been married twelve years and together for fifteen, and I felt utterly abandoned in a time of great need. Sven and Elsa became my support system, and Wanda brought us groceries and took my blood samples to the hospital. I spent most daylight hours in the bedroom, the only room with blinds, allowing me to limit the amount of sunlight. I found great comfort listening to Sven and Elsa practise their piano, often "Für Elise," and sometimes they worked on duets. Whatever they played soothed and comforted me.

Eventually, my ophthalmologist authorized me to take a road test to get my licence back. I was so terribly anxious; this was going to determine whether I could continue to live at the farm. Without my licence, I lost my independence.

A week or so before my test, Wanda once again came to my rescue. She dropped off Elsa and me at the Midtown shopping mall in Saskatoon, where Elsa patiently helped me practise stepping on and off the escalator, over and over again. Even stepping up and down a curb presented a major hurdle for me, and I could not keep my balance walking in the dark. Still today this is a challenge for me.

I cried when the instructor gave me the news that, apart from driving a little too fast at one point, which cost me two demerits, I had a perfect drive. I had my licence back. I appreciated every single day with a new energy and zest for life. Slowly, our lives began to find a new normal. Not only did I start driving again; I had to haul a trailer of livestock to the abattoir! The following year, Hans's niece came from Sweden to live with us, and I was thrilled to be able to teach her to drive. It would take me three years to recover, although nothing would ever be the same.

Prior to my stroke, Sven had pleaded with me to be home-schooled so he could spend time riding and training his horses in daylight hours. He hated the long bus drives to and from school, but now I needed someone with me at home. He switched to an on-line education program from the South Island Distance Education School in British Columbia. He became a great help to me during this very difficult time. He consistently rose to the occasion of being the man of the farm. He was responsible for all of our livestock and equipment, and he took it all in stride, never complaining, always seeming to be in heaven in his role. I felt such joy to see him in his glory.

Looking back on this time, I can see that Sven took the brunt of my sadness, and now I realize the way I leaned on him was wrong. In my defense, I don't know what else I could have done. I was so broken. Sven stayed home to support me in my healing journey for three years.

By 1996, tensions had significantly increased between Hans and the SRC. Politicians wanted letters of endorsement for a proposed synchrotron, an accelerator that produces different kinds of light in order to study the structural and chemical properties of materials at the molecular level. Hans did not support the venture. He felt the money would be better spent on providing safe drinking water solutions for rural communities. He also argued that the model they were planning would be insignificant on the world stage of synchrotrons. The politicians dictated to those running the SRC, and none of them wanted to be tarnished by Hans's pen or mouth. When he refused to sign a letter of endorsement, his job was threatened. Hans reluctantly signed the letter, which he termed a "wishy washy" excuse for a synchrotron.[13]

SRC management eventually decided Hans was no longer allowed to talk to the media. At the time, he was beginning to raise alarm bells about diquat. It would take the European Union until 2019 to no longer approve diquat, which studies now demonstrate can cause cataracts and affect the liver and kidneys if found in water or food sources at high enough levels.[14] Hans felt that remaining silent was contradictory to his role as a scientist, especially as the principal research scientist at the SRC. This marked the beginning of the end of his time with the SRC, and the beginning of our journey exposing the issues of Canada's unsafe drinking water. We had no idea what lay in store for us.

5

The Safe Drinking Water Foundation

Hans returned one night from Saskatoon and announced that he had resigned. "No way I'm accepting that ten-year pin from SRC!" Hans was dismayed that rural families were drinking disgusting, murky water, and he refused to accept that he could not make announcements to the public regarding his research.

Hans had received approximately $37,000 as his inheritance from his grandmother and with it, he started his own research and consulting business, WateResearch Corporation (WRC), and a foundation focussed on developing safe drinking water treatment systems. This was registered as a national charity, which he called the Safe Drinking Water Foundation (SDWF). Hans negotiated with the National Hydrology Research Institute and secured operating space for SDWF—in the same building where he had worked for the SRC in Saskatoon.

The SDWF began as a charity committed to improving rural water quality problems in developing countries. By this point, it was clear in the scientific literature that water-borne microorganisms could cause gastrointestinal diseases but could also lead to chronic skin infections and other diseases affecting the liver and the respiratory, cardiovascular and central nervous systems. Once we learned of the poor conditions on our own doorstep, however, we began researching the impacts of ineffective water treatment systems. At the time, Health Canada was estimating that water-borne illnesses were costing the nation around $200 million annually. Yet, as Hans wrote in 2000, if "we then add to those numbers new microbes that are added just about every month to the list of known water-borne transmissions, such as Hepatitis A virus, Coxsackie B virus, which can cause heart disease and insulin dependent diabetes, these costs are quite conservative."[15]

Hans collaborated with five other international scientists on the founding of the SDWF. One co-founder was Richard Robarts, a highly acclaimed scientist who also worked in the same building. He was the director of the United Nations Environmental Program and Global Environmental Monitoring System. When Hans and Richard wrote the founding documents, I suggested they ask a public figure to become their honourary chairperson. Pierre Trudeau was their first choice. Hans met with him at an Ontario law firm's office. They chatted around a large boardroom table and Pierre seemed sincere in his desire to support the SDWF. Soon after, he sent a letter of regret, stating that his health had deteriorated and he could not accept the position, but he would follow their work and mission closely.

We were fortunate to have well-educated and influential people join the board of the SDWF over the next few years, each with their own history that led them to the issue of safe drinking water in Canada. When Richard stepped down from the board, Hans invited Dr. David Schindler, an internationally acclaimed scientist with whom Hans had worked at Fisheries and Oceans Canada in Winnipeg, to become chairman of the board. Dave was the prominent scientist who worked on innovative large-scale experiments at the Experimental Lakes Area, where he proved that phosphorus controlled the eutrophication (or excessive algae blooms) in temperate lakes. This led to the banning of phosphates in detergents.[16]

We were also fortunate in bringing Dr. Mark Torchia to the board. Dr. Torchia had developed laser technology to treat inoperable brain tumors.[17] At a conference, Mark had met a pediatrician who worked in Northern Canada and was frustrated with the lack of safe drinking water to make formula for babies. Because formula mixed with unsafe water was dangerous and milk was exorbitantly expensive, parents had to resort to giving their children less healthy alternatives, such as juice and soft drinks. This need for clean water inspired Dr. Torchia's dream to build a small-scale treatment facility to make safe, bottled water available in all First Nations communities, where it could be used with powdered formula.

Dr. John O'Connor was another valuable board member. At the time he was a family physician practising in Fort Chipewyan, Alberta. Many of his patients suffered from rare cancers and illnesses that he attributed to their drinking water. In 2006, John called for a thorough health review of the community. His findings contributed to concerns that oil extraction operations may be contaminating the environment with carcinogenic chemicals. In what seemed to be an attempt to silence him, Health Canada lodged four complaints against John with his professional body, which put his medical licence at risk.[18] Doctors were alarmed by this incident, since such reports from doctors in the field have been vital to the detection of new diseases and public health issues. In 2007, the Canadian Medical Association passed a resolution calling for whistle-blower protection for doctors. Hans wrote an article about John's experience in the *Aboriginal Times* titled "Health Canada's Golden Rule," where he suggests "the one with the gold makes the rules."[19] I was pleased to learn that, many years later, in 2021, Ryerson University's Centre for Free Expression awarded John with the inaugural Peter Bryce Prize for Whistleblowing.[20] He said he was stunned to learn he received the award, as he didn't see himself as a whistle-blower, but rather an advocate.[21] It was this collection of concerns and experiences, among others, that were the foundation of the SDWF. We were fortunate to attract high quality and passionate individuals to the SDWF board of directors, yet government departments still did not want to hear what we were saying.

Hans suggested I become the administrator for both the WRC and the SDWF. At the time, I was teaching myself how to read all over again. When I tried to read, all the letters on the page jumped around and switched places. It was like trying to read a static alphabet that I had taken out of the dryer. I cut out small windows from a blank sheet of paper and held it over a child's kindergarten book and focussed on one word at a time. Numbers were another story. I thought a specific number, yet I wrote something quite different. Simple math became a huge challenge. I was also housebound. I greatly appreciated when Wanda took me on outings to Outlook for groceries. Otherwise, we relied on what we had in our freezers and what neighbours brought in for us. Hans felt that the administrative work would be an effective way for me to improve my office skills. I needed to regain my sense of independence, to be useful and productive again, and was eager to get back to work, although I didn't really have any other option. I made up my mind to step up to the challenge and give it my all. It was slow going. I still struggle with reading and writing twenty-seven years later.

One of my first tasks for the SDWF was to create a phone directory. I decided to use cards in a manual rolodex. After spending hours recording people, names, emails and phone numbers, I was pleased with my accomplishments. Hans was not so happy.

"What a waste of time. I won't know whether to look up anyone by their first or second name. You always confuse them and muddle them up." He reached for his old Day-timers as he spoke. He kept every one piled around his desk—and I mean every single one, going back twenty years to his university days. They were in no particular order.

He picked one at random and opened to a specific page as he declared, "See here, I know I last spoke to Bob Stewart on December 5, 1984, so all I have to do is open my calendar to that page and there is his number." He would write down the name of the person and their phone number on the date he called them. His memory could easily recall the date of the phone call, going back decades.

"Phone cards are a waste of time," he concluded. We agreed that he could keep his Day-timers, and I would keep my rolodex cards. I always knew our brains worked differently, but now I understood just how different.

That winter, through WRC, Hans accepted another contract in Thailand. Unfortunately, back at the farm, the propane gas furnace had quit working. We had a wood-burning stove to keep us

In my office, where the phone never stopped ringing with pleas for help.

warm, but we were almost out of firewood, and it took a lot of wood to heat the house 24-7 with no other source of heat. To compound our struggles, the valve at the base of our dugout froze open and we lost our water supply back to the river. Sven, Elsa and I were stranded at the farm because I had lost my driver's licence. Sven and his friend Quinn came up with an ingenious idea. Each afternoon after school, they hauled a heavy, three-inch diameter firehose down eight hundred feet of the frozen, snow-packed riverbank. They used an auger to drill a hole in the ice, placed a pump in the river, connected the hose to the pump and then pumped water to the dugout. Within three hours, the hose froze solid, and they carried the heavy, stiff line back up the bank. The boys then climbed extension ladders to drape the hoses over the roof of the barn to thaw in the next day's sun, each hose draining as it melted. The task was repeated the following day. This is how we continued to supply water to the house that winter.

Hans's early consulting work often took him to Thailand or China for months at a time. In the late nineties, he was contracted by the World Health Organization to advise the Chinese government on water treatment in an area of China with high levels of arsenic in the wells and in community drinking water. Back at home, word about Hans's work with clean and contaminated water was spreading through rural communities. I took a call from a farmer who ran eight hundred head of cattle and was concerned about the high levels of arsenic in his three wells, which provided water solely for his cattle. Each year, he sent about four hundred to be slaughtered for consumption. In one well, the level of arsenic was higher than any ever tested by the WHO in the world's worst arsenic-contaminated water supply in China.

The farmer's concern was that he had contacted two Crown corporations, SaskWater and SaskHealth, and neither of them were interested as long as humans were not drinking the water. It was not considered a problem if it were only cattle drinking the water. Yet the farmer believed his cattle were absorbing the arsenic and would pass it on to consumers eating the beef. He wondered how much arsenic his older bred cows had absorbed into their systems, and possibly passed on to their calves. The farmer ran a farm that had been handed down in his family for generations. It was their livelihood. He could not financially absorb the costs of doing the right thing: either building an adequate treatment process for his cattle's water or selling off his cattle and his farm. He continues to this day to raise cattle and send them to market. If responsible government departments deemed his situation acceptable, why should he worry?

The initial focus of Hans's research and development was growing algae. He believed it would be the world's biggest new phenomenon, a cure for ill health, the basis of enriched vitamins and the key compound in biological treatment of source waters. He consulted Dr. David Horrobin in the UK, who was launching his own private pharmaceutical research laboratory. He felt that algae and omegas produced by the algae would be the new basis for medicine; his focus was on how algae could be used in medicine to treat schizophrenia.[22] I was happy to support this venture as Hans's scientific research buddies had also recommended that I take huge doses of omegas to aid the recovery from my stroke, and it seemed to be working.

Hans negotiated to take over an extensive algae collection from Dr. Richard "Dick" Steele, a scientist he knew who lived in Bellingham, Washington. Dick and his wife, Jan, drove their motor home to visit us and hand-deliver the algae collection. Dick and Hans spent the two weeks talking about algae, and Jan and I got along famously. One afternoon during their stay, Jan began screaming for me to come to their trailer. Tony, Elsa's horse, had invited herself into the front door of their motor home and became wedged halfway up their steps! I wish I had a photo. After a great deal of tail pulling and coaxing, and with a pot of Vaseline rubbed into her flanks, she eventually backed out. Tony often waited patiently at our front door, as if waiting for the kids to come out and play.

For the algae production, Hans repurposed the trenches built for the now-finished tilapia contract, and the family came up with a plan to build a laboratory by renovating the side of our poultry barn. Hans spent considerable time on eBay buying equipment and, after reading some books on carpentry and straw bale construction,

Elsa's horse Tony, one of our beloved extended family, waits patiently at our front door.

Sven and Quinn began building. The laboratory design included gravity-fed water tanks to grow algae and easily extract it once it reached peak production. They also built fifty algae ponds using square bales of straw, lining them with strong plastic. Some were one bale in height while others were three or four, up to two metres high. The boys did a superb job over the summer. When they were finished, I bought them each a lightweight, titanium hammer that I had engraved, indicating they had earned their PhD in carpentry on the project. We had many laughs and good times, and both boys learned a great deal.

Hans applied for a grant from the National Research Council (NRC) for his algae research, and the NRC sent officials to meet him in the laboratory the boys had built. The officials were a lady in business dress and high heels and three male bureaucrats dressed in suits and ties from Ottawa. They wanted to see Hans's facility and discuss the science with him, but the meeting quickly became a mockery of science and government. The men asked endless questions about grain bins rather than algae. The lady was more interested in our daughter and her friend making jams and jellies in our kitchen. The visitors knew little about algae and it appeared to me that they wanted to change the subject. The grant was not approved.

As he planned his laboratory, Hans bought items on eBay obsessively. I recall the day a truck arrived, and the driver complained that we didn't have a loading dock to unload three skids of boxes. The driver had to manually unload the delivery and he wasn't happy about it. I wasn't happy either when I opened the first box: Hans had bought the entire clearance stock of a video store! Another time, Hans ordered five hundred pairs of winter gloves. He thought we could give them out to the homeless. Yet another time, it was five hundred disposable razors.

"I calculated how often I shave," Hans explained, "and the cost of razors is ridiculously expensive, so I bought these to last me the rest of my life."

One day I drove into town and ran into an acquaintance. She surprised me when she said, "Susan, you are the most pragmatic person I have ever known." I wasn't sure if it was a compliment or an insult. I'd always seen things as black and white, right or wrong, and this characteristic became even more ingrained and obvious following my stroke. I decided it was a compliment, something I could rely on as everything around me continued to shift.

6

Yellow Quill First Nation

In 1999, Hans was a guest speaker at the annual Canadian Institute of Public Health Inspectors conference in Saskatoon. There, he met Carla Plotnikoff, a public health inspector, who spoke with him about the relationship between drinking water quality and First Nations communities. Indigenous and Northern Affairs Canada (INAC),[23] which was responsible for water treatment in Indigenous communities, had limited solutions, and Carla was concerned that many people in the Yellow Quill community were ill and had terrible skin rashes. She believed it was caused by drinking water contaminated by spring runoff from a nearby community's sewage. Hans did not recognize the significance of her concerns at first, but Carla's diligence and relentless phone calls convinced Hans to visit the community.

He met her at the Yellow Quill community and was distraught when he returned home. He wrote about his first visit to the community in *Environmental Science and Engineering*, which I quote at length below. At the conference, Hans writes,

> [Carla] described conditions that I had only associated with developing countries. I was skeptical. I had been instrumental in forming the SDWF two years earlier. I had toured rural China and Thailand looking for drinking water issues that needed correcting. But Canada? I must admit I knew nothing about First Nation communities or issues. But, how bad could it be? We drove to Yellow Quill on

June 19, 1999, and talked to the three band councillors who demanded an end to the by then four-
year boil water advisory.

We then followed water operator Robert
Neapetung and engineering company representatives down to the water treatment plant. Robert
explained that it was necessary to open the door
of the water treatment plant and wait five to ten
minutes before going inside, as the smell of hy-
drogen sulphide was so bad. But, even when Robert thought it was okay to go inside, the plant still
smelled bad. ... Before leaving I took a sample of
the raw water coming into the water treatment
plant. Not only did it look unbelievably bad; it
reeked of rotten eggs and algae. A closer look at
the chemicals Robert used in the water treatment
plant made me very concerned. The first chemical
added to the water was Elimin-ox. This is a chemical that removes oxygen from the water in boiler
plants. It contains a chemical that is a known car-
cinogen."[24]

It was evident that Carla and Tim Bonish, the regional manager of Environmental Public Health Services at the First Nations and
Inuit Health Branch of Health Canada, had the desire to act for the
greater good of all people involved, but I think they may have had a
greater insurmountable challenge than we did at the SDWF. Hans
reviewed the numerous unsuccessful requests made by the Yellow
Quill Chief and Council, asking that INAC adequately test and treat
their water, and he vowed to do all he could to help the community.
Robert's daughter, Roberta, followed in her father's footsteps and
became the water treatment operator at Yellow Quill. Her son Blaze
became the SDWF poster child.

The more involved Hans became in reviewing analysis or
communications between First Nations leaders and civil servants
he became convinced that many politicians were indifferent to the

plight of First Nations drinking water. After discovering the terrible situation on our doorstep, I became more involved with the SDWF, and I decided that education must be part of the solution. We presumed that Canadians didn't understand or know what was happening in First Nations communities across the country, so we created the Operation Water Drop (OWD) program. I dreamed up the idea, but it was Norma, who had worked for Hans at the SRC, who developed the three water quality tests for the OWD educational program. The testing kits were sent to schools for teachers to use with their students, and students were encouraged to compare water quality in different communities, demonstrating the difference between urban and rural water supplies.

The challenge was to acquire the funding so we could get the kits into schools. Fundraising for the SDWF was a steep learning curve for me; although I had experience fundraising for the Saskatchewan Abilities Council, that was a well-known and established organization with a solid donor base. The SDWF was new and unfounded, and it was rare that anyone understood the need. Science is not easily explained to unscientific individuals. Hans and I developed a system where he wrote articles and then I reviewed them, pointing out sections where he needed to explain the science in layman's terms. At the same time, I was able to apply my business experience from Eaton's, and my organizational skills helped me manage my growing responsibilities at the SDWF. I was so thankful that my health gradually improved, giving me the strength to achieve all we did.

While hundreds of foundations had websites inviting requests for funding, few had funds available to distribute beyond what they had already committed to their selected charities. Writing fundraising proposals took hours. Each foundation had specific formats and requested financial reports that had to be extracted from financial statements.

When a new charity has little or no track record, the response is considered good if 2 to 4 percent of funding applications succeed. Once the SDWF had five years of audited financial statements, it helped to prove our persistence, and the response steadily improved. But it was slow going until that point. I submitted fundraising proposals requesting funds to test community source waters, distribute educational programs and kits and, later, to train

A student conducting an experiment with an SDWF Operation Water Drop test kit.

water treatment operators, predominantly in First Nations communities.

I entered OWD into a competition sponsored by the Green Street program, and we were humbled to be selected as a winner. Green Street was a national program funded by the McConnell Foundation and its mission was to bring environmental education programs into schools across Canada. At first, Green Street promised a three-year commitment to OWD, but it was later extended to five years. This commitment was the helping hand we needed. The Green Street stamp of approval gave us more than an introduction to other foundations; it was an endorsement that opened doors for funding in support of the distribution of even more school kits across Canada. Green Street's networking opportunities, conferences and workshops were also invaluable.

The Farm Credit Corporation was another initial donor to SDWF. With their donation, the SDWF hired a professional to build an excellent website. As we marketed our OWD kits, they were soon requested by schools across the country, and I focussed on finding donors willing to sponsor our water testing kits for schools. TD Friends of the Environment Foundation then became another source of funding, and we submitted requests to each local chapter. I soon learned that many chapters would donate funds to provide schools with water testing kits, but only in the communities where they had branches. So, I had to determine how to source funding for water testing kits to schools in rural and Indigenous communities where there were no TD branches, or if their chapter declined our request. Fortunately, several other funders would sponsor kits for these schools. There are far too many generous sponsors to name, but some that come to mind that sponsored kits for rural and Indigenous schools are the Thomas Sill Foundation, Weston Family Foundation, RBC, Saskatchewan Indian Gaming Authority, Dakota Dunes Community Development Corporation and, in later years, Mosaic.

Eventually, the SDWF offered three educational programs with kits: OWD, Operation Water Pollution and Operation Water Biology. At the time of writing, these programs are still available in French and English. The SDWF has more programs that can be downloaded for free from its website, including Operation Water Spirit and Operation Water Health (both available in French, Cree and English), Operation Water Flow (available in French and English), and Operation Community Water Footprint. The fact sheets to support these lessons are available in French and English, and those that relate to Operation Water Spirit are also available in Cree.[25]

One of the first foundations to donate in 1999 was the EJLB Foundation, and they committed to fund SDWF in later years. However, when the SDWF switched its focus from third-world countries to Indigenous communities in Canada, EJLB pulled their funding without explanation.

7

Y2K

Y2K envisioned an end to computers and technology; banks and investments were predicted to crash because the computerized clocks couldn't change from 1999 to 2000—according to the experts! It was all Hans needed to stockpile even more. Most of the time I was not aware of the full extent of all his purchases. He simply put them in the barn or the machine shed and forgot about them. Hans used the premise of Y2K as his excuse for a multitude of what seemed like outrageous purchases to me. The end of the world was fast approaching, and he was preparing, making sure we would be protected. It wasn't until years later that I realized it was a disorder and had a name: hoarding. More than ten years later, most of these boxes moved to a new home at Value Village in Saskatoon.

Hans embraced this theory to the bitter end; it was just another reason why we needed to be self-sufficient. I often went a month at a time when I couldn't get out of the farm, between blizzards, heavy snowfalls and temperatures dipping below -30 Celsius. Snow days were welcomed by the kids when the school bus couldn't run. We lived out of our four well-stocked freezers; we could have gone the entire winter without stocking up on food. Today, I am proud: I raised my children on an organic diet before it was trendy to do so.

When the clock turned to midnight, it was supposed to be the end of the world. Of course, that didn't happen. Hans never spoke of it again, just like he never referred to the many shipments he hoarded in the barn. Instead, Sven, Elsa, Hans and I lit a nice fire in our firepit, enjoyed a few drinks of Glug, a Swedish mulled wine, and some great food. I decided we should share our own ideas for what the future may hold. I gathered scraps of paper on which we wrote a question and passed it to the next person to answer. Here are a select few:

> Hans: How powerful will computers be in 2024? Today, a typical computer is 300 mHz, 100 megabytes of RAM and a 5-gigabyte hard drive.

> Sue: They'll only be as powerful as the persons operating them.

> Hans: What will I do in twenty-five years from now?

> Sue: Dad will go into semi-retirement, only working seventy hours a week, but as a national leader for safe drinking water.

> Sue: Where do you think you will live in 2024? Describe your home and surroundings.

> Sven: Cabin, a woodstove, solar power. Have nine horses, two Old English Sheepdogs, one Saint Bernard, piles of pine trees with a lake right outside my house. The moss will be a metre deep, and I'll have a thirty-six-inch television.

> Sue: If you could only take one thing with you to 2024, what would it be?

> Elsa: I would take the land which I live on. Today with nothing changed. With the river, and the house.

We welcomed a new millennium together. As so often happened, the few hours we had together every few months gave me hope of our old selves returning. Slowly, I had to learn to accept that we can never go back in time.

✖

I had always been an intuitive and sensitive person, very aware and concerned for others, but after my brain-related issues, these traits became even stronger and my need to keep busy, my coping mechanism, became more intense. Intuition had also become foremost in my decision-making, and my sense of right and wrong had increased significantly. With this came judgement and reasoning. Flashbacks and triggers became substantial; seeing an image that took me back in time, hearing a comment or a song, feeling a presence, tasting food—all these emotions could make my mind hit recall. Music could be either an offender or a calming influence, depending on the music, and I was very sensitive to sensations and stimuli. To this day, wind upsets me terribly. I easily become disoriented and my poor balance becomes an issue. Similarly, when a storm front is approaching my head physically hurts, the left side of my face freezes and I become stressed.

I have always loved soaking in a tub with a lit candle, a glass of wine and a great book. That is how I relaxed. The water at the farm was so foul we didn't linger when taking showers, let alone soak in a tub. For showers, we got wet, turned off the tap to lather up, then turned on the tap for a quick rinse, in part because water was in short supply, but mostly because the water stunk so terribly. Hans promised he would tweak the water system, that it wouldn't be a big deal, and to go ahead and order a nice soaker tub, which I did, complete with jets. The tub was installed, but Hans never improved the water system and so it was very rarely used.

I had never liked wealth or greed, but I began to despise those qualities. Material things lost their value. After all those hours, days, months of being isolated in my home, with only my own thoughts, I had no desire to own anything. But emotional things, like love, touch, and kindness, I craved more and more as each year passed.

When I had emergency surgery for a gallbladder attack, Elsa stayed with me in the hospital, and it seemed that in no time I was discharged. Luckily, Sven had his licence and was able to pick me up from the hospital. He was so thoughtful and considerate. He surprised me by telling me he had filled the bathtub, and I could take a bath. He figured this would help me unwind and relax. Once again, our water pipes were frozen, so he had carried huge buckets of water from our dugout, brought them into the house and heated them in large pots on the stove, then filled the bathtub, adding Epsom salts to the water. How I would have loved to do just that—soak in my big bathtub. He didn't know that I couldn't soak my incisions. I walked into the bathroom, looking at the dirty, discoloured water, smelling the grossness of algae. No amount of Epsom salts could have masked that odour. I felt so sorry for Sven; it was laboriously hard for him to carry all that water and heat it. He pulled the plug and let it drain away. A part of me drained away with the water. Maybe a part of him did too.

8

The Complexities of
Rural Water Sources in Canada

In the spring of 2000, residents of the sleepy town of Walkerton, Ontario, struggled with severe stomach flu symptoms. As citizens cared for children and family members, they followed doctors' advice and made sure they kept drinking water. Ironically, the more water they drank, the sicker they became. Two thousand people became sick and seven died, including a two-year-old child. Eventually, the cause was determined to be E. coli and total coliforms in the community's water supply. After an extensive investigation, Stan and Frank Koebel, the manager and foreman of Walkerton's Public Utilities Commission respectively, were formally charged with negligence. Stan was sentenced to one year in jail and Frank received nine months of house arrest.[26]

A few days before this outbreak, Hans had published an article in *Municipal World* warning about the quality of water in rural Canada, and a few days before that, he gave a presentation at a Health Canada sponsored conference where he also gave a warning. In an article for *Canadian Water Treatment,* Hans writes that Saskatchewan's Minister of Environment who was in attendance had taken "pity on developing countries with 'their water quality problems.'" Days later, Canada made international headlines for Walkerton's water crisis.[27]

Dr. Peter Huck, a professor in the civil and environmental engineering department at the University of Waterloo, claimed this was a one-time situation; "an aberration," in his exact words. Yet it was "more like 'a thousand of a kind,'" Hans writes, "as literally thousands of boil water advisories were issued by government agencies across the country in the wake of Walkerton."[28] Government agencies, Hans noted, were too quick to praise the virtues of Canadian engineering and rural treatment plants, for "nowhere in the developed world has drinking water quality been treated as casually as in Canada." He continues:

> If we have close to pristine water to treat, like some of Canada's major rivers and lakes, the current state of engineering may be considered acceptable. But with sewage and manure as well as organic material from terrestrial and aquatic vegetation tainting more rural water sources, many water treatment systems are woefully inadequate.[29]

Eventually, government agencies proposed chlorination as the solution in Walkerton. Sales of chlorine drastically increased across the nation and communities were issued coliform tests. Communities that had water that didn't pass the test were issued boil water advisories. Yet, as Hans has written elsewhere, "if a community has raised its chlorine levels and coliform bacteria persist you know that you have major problems with your water," for bacteria like E. coli and coliform are usually killed long before other serious disease-causing viruses and parasites.[30]

Hans and I listened to media coverage of the Walkerton crisis, which included much discussion as to whether education would have avoided the issue. "No," Hans objected, cynically, whenever this question was raised. "Education would simply have enabled them to do a better job of covering up their negligence. If someone has no conscience, education is not going to change anything." In his *Canadian Water Treatment* article, he was scathing:

> provinces that have trouble spelling the names of some microbes are supposed to be the "experts" dealing with the illnesses they cause. [...] It is not until we start dealing with real drinking water issues

including parasites and viruses that the skills of
engineering companies and government agencies
will be known. But, until then, rural water users
are well advised to take better precautions than
what their local municipal water treatment plant
affords them.[31]

Bruce Davidson was a citizen of Walkerton when his family
became ill from this tragedy. He founded Concerned Citizens of
Walkerton and became a close ally of the SDWF. The lawyer representing the town of Walkerton spoke at the inquiry about the value
of lives lost. I watched the trial on the television from home, and
my stomach churned when I heard the lawyer, referring to the two-
year-old child who had died, implying that the life of a two-year-old
isn't worth very much. Perhaps my memory is distorting the an-
guish I felt at that time, but his comments were forever embedded
in my mind. His premise was that the value of any life was based on
lost income: a two-year-old child did not earn an income, so their
life was of little or no value. If we want to sink to this abhorrent
logic, I can see it applied in the opposite sense: a two-year-old child
lost a lifetime of potential earnings, the maximum of any claimant.

He was also, of course, implying a hierarchy of worth between
adult individuals: he inherently suggested that an unemployed Indigenous person had less value than a (white) lawyer. I wonder, is
this logic at the root of the few improvements to safe drinking water
for Indigenous Peoples since 1997? I feel that in the eyes of some
individuals, some lives simply are less worthy than others.

For some affected by this tragedy, it never faded away. Robbie
Schnurr, a citizen of Walkerton, ended his life on Tuesday, May 1,
2018, through medically assisted dying. He lived with severe neu-
rological damage following his poisoning by the Walkerton water in
2000. His legs slowly wasted away over eighteen years. Numbness
in his fingers made it impossible for him to write or button a shirt;
he opened bottles of painkillers with his mouth. Robbie lost the
sight in his right eye; the hearing in one ear was already gone. He left
his home every two weeks, strapped on a gurney for transportation to

the Queensway Health Centre for an intravenous immunoglobulin treatment. He went for the last time in late April of 2018.[32]

The city of North Battleford, Saskatchewan, suffered a similar situation to Walkerton one year later. The city hosted an international dance competition over a spring weekend in 2001, and as the participants were on their way home, severe flu symptoms surfaced among the competition's participants and the city's residents. Over seven thousand people—nearly half of the city's population—became ill. The city issued a three-month boil water advisory.[33] Once again, various media representatives called on Hans for his perspective.

Doctors co-ordinated multiple lab tests to confirm the source of the problem. Hans observed that the Saskatchewan provincial lab results came back with mostly negative results, yet labs around the world came back with a high ratio of positive test results. Attempting to minimize the situation, then Mayor Wayne Ray and then Environment Minister Buckley Belanger posed for a photo while drinking tap water from Styrofoam cups.[34]

Hans was very outspoken, and he raised these questions to media. "Was the science in the Saskatchewan laboratories flawed? Was there a conspiracy to deflate the issue? Were the labs in Saskatchewan incompetent?"

Three lawsuits connected to the crisis would unfold in the years to follow. Hans's position on the situation was documented as he was called to be an expert witness to the provincial inquiry. The province of Saskatchewan settled out of court, which spoke volumes for where the faults lay.

The positive lab results revealed the parasite cryptosporidium, which can cause a disease called cryptosporidiosis, or "crypto."[35] A few weeks before individuals started reporting their symptoms, the city's water treatment plant—located two kilometres downstream from the city's sewage plant—received some maintenance work. At the time, the province was inspecting the treatment facility once every ten years. Inadequate and infrequent procedures, and its proximity to the sewage plant, left the facility vulnerable. Indeed, in the wake of the Walkerton outbreak a year prior, the provincial government received a warning that a similar issue was on the horizon for North Battleford, according to documents leaked in 2001.[36] Thankfully, no one died from the outbreak, but the town was lucky: in 1993, cryptosporidium was found in Milwaukee's drinking water, and 400,000 people (half the city's population) became ill and more than one hundred people died. The accumulated costs for this incident reached $25 billion USD.[37] Hans was fuelled to pen more critical articles, which opened doors for more publications that wanted to publish his opinions.

Civil servants with good hearts tried to do what they could in a broken system. Jouko Kurkiniemi was one rare person. Working for INAC, he was responsible for First Nations water quality in Saskatchewan. Jouko was fortunate that his boss, Earl Kreutzer, was equally committed to doing the right thing for First Nations. Together, they made things happen. In 2002, Jouko Kurkiniemi gave WRC a research and development contract to work on Yellow Quill First Nation's community groundwater problems. As we would eventually discover, hundreds of First Nations, Inuit and Métis communities suffered the same, or worse, drinking water problems. At the time, we did not know what a huge and daunting task Hans would be taking on with this contract. His three-month project took two years. The hard work was about to begin, and I had no idea how this would affect our family.

That summer, Sven and Quinn retrofitted a semi-trailer for Hans to use as a pilot mobile laboratory. This was ready to drive to Yellow Quill First Nations community, three hundred kilometres east of Saskatoon. The laboratory had electrical conduit and plumbing around the perimeter of the interior walls, and six of each of the largest possible membranes and plastic containers that fit into the trailer.

We decided to paint a mural on the side of the trailer to publicize the SDWF and its mission. I began searching locally, but after a few failed attempts to secure someone permanent, it was made clear to me that connecting with Indigenous artists who were unable to support themselves in a small rural community was a challenge.

One man spent a day working on the project, but despite my efforts to assist with transport, he did not return to finish the work. Another man who had proudly found his passion for art while in prison, was similarly unable to commit to multiple days of work. Beyond logistics, both men were dealing with personal demons connected to their experiences as Indigenous men in Canada.

We were running out of time before we needed to move the trailer to Yellow Quill, so Elsa used a ladder to paint an amazing eagle, and together we finished the painting. The trailer left our yard on a Tuesday; I remember the day vividly. Ten days before this, I had learned that my father was diagnosed with terminal lung cancer, and the doctors gave him two months to live. I booked my flight to Winnipeg to spend time with him, but I had to get the trailer on its way before I could leave the next day. Sadly, my father passed away that night and I didn't get to say goodbye.

Hans decided to live in a large army tent at Yellow Quill, a four-to-five-hour drive from the farm. I was in a terribly confused mindset. I loved salvaging any part of his caring soul, the caring soul I fell in love with, so when Hans was leaving us to help resolve these horrific drinking water issues, I was proud of him. I held a genuine desire to help too. At the same time, I was bitter, bitter that he had abandoned me, bitter that I didn't get to say goodbye to my father when he passed quite suddenly, bitter that our kids didn't grow up in the loving family I thought we had. I was a bitter woman. But in true stoic British form, I bottled up my pain, kept it inside and soldiered on. Hans would leave Yellow Quill and return home once or twice a year during those two years.

As each month passed, it became more obvious that this project was an enormous challenge. Jouko and Earl never questioned Hans needing more time; they, like me, had complete faith in his ability to design an effective system.

We learned early on the importance of building personal trust and respect in our relationships with First Nations leaders. Many began calling, each hopeful their community could benefit from the same process Hans was developing at Yellow Quill. They all had stories of despicable water—the stench of rotten eggs, the colour of slime or waste, of boil water advisories, not for months or even years, but for decades. They shared heart-wrenching stories of ill health and skin diseases that they believed were caused by their poor water quality. Word spread between communities, at first within Saskatchewan, then throughout Ontario and Alberta. It wasn't just the stories of the water and the health issues that wrenched at my heart, but the repeated indifference of responsible government agencies and engineers, individuals who were paid, and very well, for building ineffective treatment systems. Each caller shared similar emotions, those of being neglected, abandoned, unheard and used to make money for the businesses of colonizers.

While I was complaining about my life, I realized that my challenges were so insignificant compared to those of the Indigenous people calling me. The more I tried to help them, the less I felt hard done by. We wanted to help them all, so I bought more semi-trailers.

The trailers had little road life left but enough to move to alternate locations. Because the weather was becoming too severe for Hans to live in the army tent, Sven and Quinn worked nights and weekends to turn a second trailer into living quarters. If a trailer had refrigeration, better known as a reefer unit, it was easy to remove the refrigeration unit and install a window in its place, ideal for living quarters. A partition was added to the bedroom beneath the window, as well as a kitchen, a shower in the centre and a living room that also functioned as an office. The boys added another window where the back doors once were, as well as parquet hardwood flooring and a freezer for Hans's food supply. The first trailer built for living accommodations left in October, and Hans did not come home until Christmas Day. Hans was living, sleeping and eating water treatment. He was developing a biological water treatment system.

Hans returned to Yellow Quill on Boxing Day. I remained at home, looking after all administrative tasks, our two children and the farm with all our livestock. At the time, we were selling farm gate—beef, poultry, sometimes turkeys, pork and lamb. We were also still growing algae, and when Hans left the farm, Elsa and I had to carefully check the algae ponds hourly.

We followed Hans's directions on how to maintain and establish the growth ponds, as well as how to harvest algae. These were my notes from the five-second crash course on how to grow algae, which Hans gave us before he left the farm:

> Use the pH metre and check pH of each pond at noon each day. If the pH is below 6.5, the algae has too much gas. Remove gas and watch carefully, monitoring pH hourly to see when it improves. If pH is between 6.5 and 7, don't put the gas on. If pH is between 7 and 7.5, check again in two hours, can put the gas on very low. But still check it again every two hours. If pH is 7.5 to 8 put the gas on, it shouldn't go over 8 though, watch it carefully to make sure and get it back down if it does.

Elsa and I worked hard on the algae ponds day after day. The area was too large to monitor hourly, and it soon became apparent that we were not born to be algae producers. The gas Hans referred to was the amount of oxygen the algae produced. What he believed to be simple we found challenging. Within a month, we killed his entire collection.

While Hans developed the ultimate water treatment system for Yellow Quill, our water at home became more foul smelling. What little water we had was full of sediment and we hated taking showers in it. Once Elsa had her driver's licence, she seized the opportunity to take a shower at a friend's home before school each day.

Still, I looked forward to my Saturday nights at home. I always saved my laundry for Saturday nights, and I always loved ironing. I showered, put on some nice clean clothes and makeup, turned on Randy Bachman and began ironing to my heart's content. I drifted back in time, wondering how I got from working my first job as an artist in an advertising agency in London, England, to a buyer for Eaton's to a remote farm in Saskatchewan. I thought about the varied people I had met, memories of attending live music shows, reliving the fashions of my day... all so far away, but for an hour or two on Saturday nights, I could relive, pretend my life was different. And carry on.

9

Canada's First IBROM Water Treatment System

As volunteer administrator for the SDWF, my creative spirit was fulfilled by developing the school programs. As I learned more about education systems through OWD, I was surprised to learn that while one province might teach certain subjects in grade five, another may teach it in six or seven, and sometimes in four. The curriculum varied significantly across Canada, and if students moved to other provinces, they could repeat classes or miss them. I believed there was an opportunity for increased interaction and applied learning using our water testing kits. I applied every spring to Human Resources and Development Canada for funding to hire university students who were studying education. Selecting suitable candidates was a challenge as many were worthy. While I dreamed up ideas to develop more school programs, the education students seized opportunities to put their knowledge and passion for learning into developing the new curriculum. I loved the brainstorming sessions as they initiated so many creative ideas. With these students, I developed programs that incorporated skills such as public speaking, persuasive writing, reading and calculating figures related to water usage and the science of water testing.

I tried to hire Indigenous students as often as possible. One lovely young lady came from Yellow Quill, and she was so sympathetic to other communities asking for help. She had earned her degree from the First Nations University of Canada in Regina. I soon discovered she needed a boost to improve her self-esteem and confidence, so I arranged some role-playing, including making phone calls and presentations. She excelled in first-hand experiences and became one of our top students.

While we were developing these programs, I uncovered some blatantly racist procedures within the government. Citizens living in rural or urban communities fell under provincial jurisdiction. They were allocated a certain amount of water per day when constructing or retrofitting water treatment facilities. First Nations communities fell under federal government and, at the time we were developing the early education programs, First Nations were allocated about 30 percent less water per day than rural citizens. Similarly, during this time, the federal government gave approximately 30 percent less funding per student to schools on reserves compared to what provincial governments gave to schools in urban or rural communities.[38] Today, these numbers are more aligned for current students, but this disparity surely left an impact, and possibly contributed the feeling of being second-class citizens for many First Nations people.

Hans continued to work closely with water treatment operators while developing the biological water treatment process. As a temporary solution, he was developing a portable system whereby any source water could be treated to produce clean water for distribution to a community in twenty-litre bottles. Sven and Quinn, once again, modified a few twenty-foot trailers to accommodate the treatment systems, which we then shipped to communities anywhere there was road access. Until we could install permanent solutions, residents could pick up their water from the mobile unit. We quickly realized their great potential: mobile units could become solutions for communities with boil water advisories and for the hundreds more that should have been on boil water advisories but weren't. The cost of providing adequate distribution to each home was exorbitant, but the mobile treatment systems could have been cost-effective and immediate, rectifying many terrible health issues. Dr. Mark Torchia was a huge proponent of this development.

Sadly, the powers in high places refused it outright. We could have implemented it at each First Nations community without effective water treatment systems, except there was no political will to do so. We presented it to INAC, but it fell on deaf ears. No matter how many phone calls I made, no matter how high up the chain of command I went, my inquiries were never responded to. We had no other option but to believe it was not fitting with INAC's agenda. What other excuse could there be?

After two years at Yellow Quill, Hans finalized the first Integrated Biological Reverse Osmosis Membrane (IBROM) water treatment system in Canada. The IBROM was field tested over twenty-two months on some of the poorest raw water sources Hans could ever have imagined.[39] He explained to laypeople like me that the IBROM system functioned like a biological "smorgasbord" designed to eat whatever needed to be removed from the problem water. He based the process off the food chain: the water would be siphoned into a membrane containing algae. Protozoa and other bacteria were then added in the chain of membranes, always beginning with the smallest bacterium and working up to larger compounds. He selected the bacteria based on the mineral or compound he wanted to remove from the water. This process removes a host of compounds and elements including gases (which can contribute to the rotten egg smell), ammonium, arsenic, organics and manganese. Lastly, the water was then run through a reverse osmosis system, effective only once all the particles in the water were removed and which removes whatever the previous process could not. The process produces water so pure it needs to be filtered through calcium and magnesium to increase the pH and add beneficial nutrients.

It was a small-scale treatment process that could easily be duplicated for communities of up to five thousand people. It was cost effective, but that caused opposition from engineering companies, who wanted to keep billing INAC for the same ineffective systems (most often sand filtration) they had built for decades. These companies benefitted from the contracts awarded by INAC, so the majority did what they could to obstruct Hans's new system. I have never heard of a scientist being involved in the planning of any water treatment plants that various engineering companies built for INAC.

Nor am I aware of INAC accurately testing source or treated water from the ineffective systems they paid engineers to build. Instead, before the IBROM, community leaders would contact Hans, Hans told them which analyses should be run on their source and treated waters, then I arranged for these samples to be sent to me. I sent them to the SRC for testing, without disclosing the name of the community, simply labelling them "Sample ABC."

It was simpler and more profitable to tweak existing plans from other communities and keep building the same ineffective systems that produced unsafe drinking water. In an article for *The Globe and Mail*, Matthew McClearn calls this the "'design, build and bugger off'" practice: contractors build ineffective systems on First Nations land and then disappear.[40] If this was a private, non-government venture, the contract would have to include the exact scientific make-up of the source water, and what levels were required to improve the water. Can we blame the engineers for taking advantage of contracts with no specifications or means to measure the effectiveness of their systems?

Following tests administered by Health Canada on treated water from the IBROM system, Hans made many phone calls asking for their decision, but they seemed to delay their inevitable approval. Hans raised the question to them on the phone, "How come you don't take this much time and effort to test all the ineffective water treatment systems that are in operation?" Hans felt that the delay in their decision could be attributed to them being disappointed that they could not find fault with the system. Soon after the IBROM became operational, Health Canada insisted that a little chlorine had to be added to the treated water. Many people in Indigenous communities didn't like the odour or the effects of chlorine.

At Yellow Quill, Robert Neapatung, the water treatment operator, took immense pride in learning the new method of water treatment. His daughter, Roberta, as well as Debbie Roper, were two young women who also became water treatment operators in their community. The operators understood the IBROM process; it was natural and organic. The water treatment operators quickly learned the biological processes and the science behind the treatment, as well as their technical roles. All the water treatment operators whom Hans trained took their responsibilities seriously, providing their communities with safe drinking water every day. Their competence supports the value of hands-on learning and speaks to how robust the IBROM systems are. In a *Prince Albert Grand Council Tribune* article, Yellow Quill Councillor Verna Cachene claimed that "skin rashes, which were so common at Yellow Quill, disappeared when the new IBROM treatment plant was taken into service. I am certain there were other health benefits in individuals which were not as apparent as a direct result of clean drinking water."[41]

I visited the Yellow Quill community sometime after their IBROM system became operational. While I was there, residents from surrounding communities had stopped by, empty water jugs in hand. The water treatment plant operators happily filled their empty jugs, sharing their safe drinking water with their neighbours. It was a heart-warming moment for me to witness.

Hans, knowing the state of the water coming in from INAC-funded systems, often took INAC to task as to why they had not run analyses on treated water before signing off on upgraded systems. To my knowledge, INAC never responded. He called the water treatment plants designed by engineers that were awarded the INAC contracts "a dog's breakfast." Here is an excerpt from an article he wrote in *Prince Albert Grand Council Tribune* referring to the engineers who had benefitted, twice, from INAC contracts:

> Take the water treatment plant that I had called a "dog's breakfast." An engineering company at that time had spent $1 million designing the "dog's breakfast." Shortly thereafter I got a contract to run an IBROM pilot. It worked well. Yet to my utter disbelief, the Band had selected to retain the engineering company and spent another $1 million. Wow! An engineering company earning another million to fix up their own design blunder! When nobody can understand your black magic,

you can get away with something like that. This community can thank its lucky stars that Jouko pushed an IBROM through after the community hired a different engineering company. Jouko felt bad that Indian Affairs [INAC] had done such a poor job technically evaluating both the first and second INAC $1 million expenditures. Jouko warned the "dog's breakfast" engineering company to never ever try to pull such a fast one on him again. Earl Kreutzer was not happy about another water treatment plant and commented about it: "The engineering company should be ashamed of itself; Indian Affairs has a long memory."

We have other examples where engineering companies have tried to pull fast ones on Indian Affairs. The engineering companies proposing to use totally inappropriate technologies and then expecting that Indian Affairs not having the technical resources (this is for sure partly true) to properly evaluate their proposals... From an engineering perspective this is actually the most profitable scenario. First, get paid for designing something that will not work. Then get called back, to spend months to try to get the water treatment plant to run. Finally, install an IBROM.[42]

I suspect that the drive for profit and power is the primary reason these engineers are awarded INAC contracts in the first place: I witnessed elections in a few communities, where those running for Chief and Council look for donors. The first to step forward with cash were engineers wanting to receive contracts for projects, often water treatment projects. Of course, these arrangements aren't limited to certain communities. While INAC has the final call, there seems to be an unwritten law that the engineering company donating to the community is awarded the pie, implying that contract assignments have little to do with actually building effective treatment systems. I wonder if this is really any different from our colonial politics. Hans revisited this power imbalance in the next article he published in the *Tribune*:

> How can totally inadequate water treatment processes be recommended to a community? Here is how: 90% of buying decisions for a new water treatment plant is made by Indian Affairs and the engineering company. 10% of those decisions are made by the First Nation. Yet it is community members in the First Nation that get to drink the water for the next 20 to 30 years. I believe that it is only when those numbers are reversed will there be enough care in the selection of both water treatment process and engineering company. 90% of those decisions should be made by the First Nation. Tops 10% for the engineering company and Indian Affairs."[43]

From what I witnessed, these percentages can fluctuate, depending on how much remains of the "Indian Agent" mentality, the level of intimidation by INAC and by engineers, as well as the ability of chiefs and councillors to stand up for their rights. Thankfully, First Nations leaders are quickly learning how to stand up against the status quo. The next step has been too long coming, but finally First Nations will be responsible for their own drinking water.

10

Saddle Lake Cree Nation

While Hans lived and worked at Yellow Quill First Nation, Tony Steinhauer, a water treatment operator at Saddle Lake Cree Nation, became a regular caller. Tony's stories were heartbreaking, and his passion to provide safe drinking water to his community was second to none. Within his immediate family, young women had lost babies, either by miscarriage or still birth, and an Elder required kidney dialysis and had to travel to Edmonton three times a week. His expenses were paid by the government, but his time and stress were not considered. This same Elder and his wife had fostered and adopted eighteen children. He deserved better. They all deserved better.

Dr. David Schindler was an eminent scientist, recipient of the Stockholm Water Prize and chairman of the SDWF board. After visiting Saddle Lake Cree Nation, he made the following statement:

> I've never seen a water supply in such poor shape. The lake is covered with blue greens, which make mats in nearshore areas. Yet, this is a drinking water supply for several thousand First Nation people! That is a story that city people need to hear and see. They cannot imagine that we have water problems of this magnitude in Alberta.[44]

In addition to Health Canada's routine tests, Saddle Lake Cree Nation conducted tests with Hans's help and scientific direction. Based on the test results, Chief and Council called a boil water advisory against the wishes of Health Canada but under Hans's advice and recommendation from the Canadian Environmental Law Association, a non-profit legal aid clinic. Months later, Health Canada was made aware of the BWA, finally opting to conduct more extensive tests on the water; they decided it was necessary to call a BWA after all.[45]

This was not an isolated incident. Six Nations of the Grand River, one of the largest First Nations reserves in Canada, experienced similar health problems and lack of due diligence by Health Canada. Health Canada tested the Nation's water in 1997, and every test demonstrated contamination. Health Canada, however, only notified the people whose wells were tested, not the whole community. In an article for *Aboriginal Times,* Hans asks, "If we see general contamination of wells, is it not prudent to alert the community to this fact? Does every house need to be tested and have E. coli found in the drinking water before Health Canada acts?"[46] The Six Nations Chief and Council hired a consultant to conduct another test, and this again demonstrated that most wells had either coliforms or E. coli contamination. As Hans writes, "It turns out failing septic tanks and ill-protected wells (from vermin, etc.) are the norm rather than the exception. One would think that Health Canada would be able to address basic sanitation issues in Native communities, yet contamination persists."[47]

After months of Tony's pleading for help at Saddle Lake, INAC gave Hans a contract to build a new IBROM. While the Yellow Quill source water was groundwater, Saddle Lake's source water was from a lake, so he would have to devise a new system. The lake was inundated with so much dissolved material (a mixture derived primarily from the decomposition of plant material, bacteria and algae) that, during windy days, the tops of the water became foamy peaks. Hans had never seen anything like it. We moved the pilot and housing trailers to Saddle Lake Cree Nation, northeast of Edmonton.

It was around the time that we were setting up at Saddle Lake that Hans called me with an SOS: his vision was blurry and he had a terrible headache. He couldn't drive the rest of the way home. Once we got him to a hospital, he was diagnosed with detached retinas in both eyes. He lost sight in one eye, but they saved the sight in the other. This was a complication of his diabetes.

Without skipping a beat, Hans continued his obsession of providing safe drinking water to communities in need. Once again, he lived, ate and breathed safe drinking water on site. He was in the same, familiar living arrangement, with the same pilot laboratory, but there were new people to train and a new source of water to treat. As before, he came home maybe one or two days a year.

Hans had a hard time keeping anything clean, evidenced by his living accommodation, the pilot lab, machine shed, the equipment stored outdoors, and the massive cartons of items he had bought on eBay and never opened. He could never find anything. Hans claimed his time was too valuable to undertake mundane tasks like cleaning. He claimed his busyness and erratic behaviour, or "scrambling" as he called it, made him important and successful, whereas I saw it as a sign of poor planning and judgement.

On one of my visits to Saddle Lake, Tony and his mentor, an Elder named Howard Cardinal, took me on a tour of the community. The large community centre had a long wall where they hung framed portraits of all the chiefs. I was mesmerized.

When I was a thirteen-year-old schoolgirl growing up on a low-income housing estate in the suburbs of greater London in the UK, I first learned about Canada. That year, Mrs. Lindsay taught us how to sew a needlework picture and various embroidery stitches, and I created a large, framed portrait of a First Nations chief in full headdress. Despite its crudeness, it was made with love, admiration and respect. I had no knowledge then of the atrocities, or political correctness. But something had drawn me to Canada, and I inevitably felt I was where I was meant to be.

✴

We had begun hearing from acquaintances connected to INAC, as well as those working in the water treatment plants, that salesmen for the chemical companies were objecting to the IBROM system: they would lose significant revenue if their chemicals were no longer needed. A community could incur costs of over $100,000 annually for these chemicals. And indeed, their chemicals were no longer needed, at least not in the same quantities. Saddle Lake Cree Nation was spending $15,000 per month in chemical costs to treat its water, but Hans was devising a system that replaced the community's previous chemical treatment and ultrafiltration with his IBROM system, which could cut chemical costs to less than $1,000 a month. And because the IBROM process feeds the water through a calcium and magnesium mineral bed as the final step, the water is not only safe to drink; it also provides essential nutrients like calcium and magnesium. Additionally, the community's boil water advisory could be lifted. Of this development, Hans wrote, "it is time to start seriously teaching biology at Canada's engineering schools."[48]

Hans explained the process simply this way: What would you rather drink, a glass of brown water or a glass of clear water? We can add chlorine to the glass of brown water and it will become clear, but a chemical analysis of the water would show that this is bad drinking water. In contrast, the clear water is of high quality, and straight chlorination of this water could make it meet all current global regulations.

In an article titled "Chemical Limitations of Groundwater Treatment" about the Yellow Quill project, Hans got to the point about chemicals. Firstly, he says, "often groundwater sources are analyzed with the main objective of compliance to guidelines. This is great if you want to comply with guidelines, but if you want to produce safe drinking water, a different approach is required."[49] An analysis of Yellow Quill's raw groundwater demonstrated that arsenic levels were well above the current guideline, as were calcium, iron, manganese and sulphate. The guidelines recommend a sulphate level of 500 mg/L, and Yellow Quill's was 1,100 mg/L. "Without sulphate removal," Hans writes, the water source "would be distinctly 'laxative.'" Following guidelines, many treatment plants are devised with the intention of removing iron and manganese from the water source, "ignor[ing] everything else," but engineers advise treatment operators to use a level of potassium permanganate that could never have a positive effect on iron or manganese. "Even with an incredibly dedicated operator, doing the chemically impossible is simply not possible!"[50] These are Band-Aid solutions—just like when the government recommended the use of chlorine to Walkerton in 2000.

Indeed, improvements since Walkerton, Hans writes,

> have mainly centered around larger and better monitored chlorine additions with less work focussing on the need for better water treatment technologies... Native Canada and INAC have done an excellent job improving operator training and certification. But, it really doesn't matter how well the operators are trained if they are forced to use tea strainers when, at a minimum, they should be using coffee filters.
>
> There are some exceptions to the above, and INAC's efforts at Yellow Quill [...] have led the way to gain a better understanding of the challenges communities are facing and what is required to resolve those challenges. Yearly removals of treated water reservoir sludge layers have become a thing of the past. In February 2004, after the reservoir cleanup at Yellow Quill, we tossed a quarter into each treated water reservoir; even at full reservoir levels (3.3 to 3.6 m[etres]) they can be seen as clearly today as when they were tossed in four years ago. This is what the federal government should be doing—helping in the search for real solutions.[51]

11

The Futility of Safe Drinking Water Guidelines

In 2004, the SDWF organized a national conference in Saskatoon. The focus was on biological filtration for water treatment, its cost effectiveness and how the process was embraced by various First Nations. Hans approached potential presenters, and the organizing, funding and promotion tasks were left to me. We had no government funding, only private support, so it was a big job to pull off. We were grateful for all the help we received from dedicated volunteers, including doctors, water treatment plant operators, scientists, engineers and concerned citizens. Hans negotiated with INAC to offer water treatment operators credits toward continued learning if they attended some of the hands-on courses. More than two hundred people attended, but we felt sure that the number would have been closer to seven hundred if all of the Indigenous people's requests to INAC for funding to attend the conference had been approved. Because government departments refused to fund many individuals working in water treatment so they could attend our conference, I recorded the entire event. Soon afterwards, I had DVDs produced and made available for a token cost to anyone interested in learning from these international speakers. We distributed hundreds of complete sets, predominantly to Indigenous communities.[52]

Tom BK Goldtooth, executive director of Indigenous Environmental Network, a grassroots environmental organization based in the US, accepted my invitation and opened our event with a powerful, resonating Indigenous chant honouring the people of Yellow

Quill First Nation. There were speeches from David Suzuki, Jack Layton, Dr. Paulette Tremblay (Six Nations of the Grand River), Bruce Davidson (a citizen of Walkerton and founder of Concerned Citizens of Walkerton), Dr. Derek Chitwood (Partners in Hope) and Dr. Colin Fricker (Independent Water Treatment Consultant). Scientists presented their research using terms that everyone could understand. Presentations focussed on how people cope with water-borne diseases in both developed and developing countries. Jack was sincere in his speech; he empathized with Indigenous people, he wanted and intended to improve the quality of drinking water on all reserves. I dream of the world we would have were he still alive.

Dr. Fricker, a water quality specialist from the UK, was often contracted to fix water treatment plants around the world. He was on the ground during the cryptosporidium outbreak in Sydney, Australia. Dr. Fricker began his presentation with a question: "If you have no coliforms or E. coli in your drinking water, what does it mean?" He posed the answer: "It means that you have met regulatory requirements. Does it mean that you have produced safe drinking water? Absolutely not! If you only take one thing from my presentation today, let it be that testing for guidelines does nothing to protect public health."[53] I will never forget the silence that blanketed the large conference room following this statement: Canada's safe drinking water guidelines were effectively futile.

Indeed, Canada was (and still is) the only developed country without national *regulations* regarding drinking water quality; we only have national *guidelines*. Imagine what would happen if we had guidelines instead of regulations for driving on highways! Hans explained this issue in a paper he co-authored with Dr. Fricker:

> The question of what needs to be done to move toward safe drinking water is not as simple as most people assume. It is a question that can have both a political and a technical answer. First, if we look at the Canadian Drinking Water Quality Guidelines, it is the result of negotiations between provincial

and federal agencies and the guidelines are really a mix of political and technical solutions. When Health Canada studied the effects of cancer-causing trihalomethanes (THMs), it was concluded that the level should be decreased from 350 to 50 micrograms/litre (µg/L). But several provinces balked at this, and a compromise level of 100 µg/L was set. The United States Environmental Protection Agency (USEPA) set the level at 80 µg/L. Several agencies are now considering below 50 µg/L levels. Political or technical?[54]

While the federal government is responsible for providing safe drinking water for First Nations communities, provincial governments are responsible for the safe drinking water in their respective provinces, for both urban and rural dwellers. One would need to ask the politicians and civil servants who blocked every initiative we created why we don't have national drinking water regulations. It all seemed so logical, so necessary and cost effective.

Rural folks still didn't seem concerned yet, aside from a few cases like the farmer with arsenic in his cattle water. Sadly, the resources were not available to address their similar challenges with drinking water.

Most of the SDWF board attended the conference. It was a rare opportunity for the board members to meet in person and discuss the future of the SDWF. We arranged campers and set up housing for everyone to stay at the farm. Following the conference, the board met to debrief. Two strong statements emerged from everyone's heartfelt discussion: first, the SDWF believed that it could facilitate the ability of individuals and communities to take responsibility and develop capacity to ensure sustainable safe drinking water. Second, we knew that all plans for development had to be based on scientific expertise. There were many points raised about the fact that science was being abused instead of used in the ability to produce safe drinking water. One person wrote on the flip chart "Bureaucrats don't think, they just DO."

Everyone present was unanimous that the SDWF could do more to effect change from outside of government than the people elected could do from within. With exception of a few individuals who were prepared to go out on a limb and risk their careers in the process, it appeared there was such indifference within the civil service to do what was right for the greater good. Everyone present was unanimous that science had to be the solution.

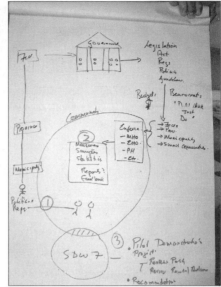

Notes on a flip chart at an SDWF board meeting, showing frustration at government inaction.

At the end of the weekend, I was significantly worn out from organizing the conference and board meeting, as well as hosting and supplying food for the board members at the farm, although I was impressed by how they all pitched in, cooked various dishes and helped clean up. (I still enjoy replicating Dr. Charl Badenhorst's South African dish of garlic beans and mashed potatoes!)

I was also emotionally drained when one of the board members ran over my daughter's dog, Freya. The dog was sleeping beside the driveway when the board member drove in and reversed without checking behind his camper. I ran to her side. She was still conscious, yet I knew her injuries were fatal. I hate guns, always have and always will, and I refused to have one on the farm. I called my dear neighbours, who dropped what they were doing to come to my side, their rifle across the back window of their farm truck, ready to euthanize her. In the end, the gun wasn't needed; Freya died in my arms. I could have easily lost my temper with that board member. He didn't help matters when he told me it was the third time that he had killed someone's dog in a similar way.

Freya was always at my daughter's side, eating the low-lying fruit while Elsa picked raspberries, or swimming beside her in the river. Freya would also always nurse another dog's pups. She was a feisty, amazing dog, and she was gone. I was devastated, my mind preoccupied during our board discussions, wondering how I would break the news to Elsa, who was travelling in Europe.

In addition, I was witnessing Hans's failing health at an alarming rate. He still refused to take medication for his diabetes, and I was concerned that there were more complications emerging in addition to the detached retinas. On the rare occasion that Hans came home, he loved to venture into the river, even if it meant breaking the ice to swim. He mocked me because I couldn't tolerate the cold, but in later years I realized this was a sign of his diabetes' progression: he was losing feeling in his extremities. His declining health was causing me great stress. I wanted board members to assume more responsibility and free up some of Hans's time, but it was a hard sell. We decided Hans needed a scientific assistant, and we hired one, but Hans was difficult to work with. Within a year, the assistant moved on and was not replaced.

Working with Hans was like trying to operate in the eye of a tornado, or perhaps a hurricane. He was always *scrambling* to accomplish everything, juggling many projects and jiggling every limb in his body while he worked. He was always late, always retracing his steps, one last thing to add, one more task to complete, "Oh, I almost forgot, I just have to…" It was impossible to keep up with him. His energy and knowledge permeated every cell of my body. His mind could always offer a rational façade; he could persuade anyone to believe he was a financial wizard, while at the same time he practised excessive spending on what I thought were ridiculous items he found online. He could always twist his point of view to present it as though he was doing someone, usually me, a great favour—just as he did when he suggested I take on the volunteer administration for the charity and business. He was creating this role to help me.

Very little revenue was coming into WRC at this time. Hans and I believed that everyone had the right to safe drinking water, but Hans took it further as he often volunteered his services. While INAC paid him to develop and design effective water treatment systems, he was never reimbursed for the hours of support and guidance he willingly gave to anyone who requested help. Hans was consistently mentoring First Nations leaders in negotiations with INAC (and standing up to their seemingly political indifference) by helping communities establish bylaws to protect and improve their drinking water. First Nations communities were not allowed to pass any bylaws unless INAC approved of them. I felt INAC often acted like ghosts of past Indian Agents. This required a tremendous amount of time spent reading reports and examining water analyses. When Hans presented substantial and accurate science, he could identify the inaccuracies that led to INAC denying the communities justice and access to safe drinking water. With the combination of stresses from finances, work, Hans's health, the strain on our marriage and my recovery from traumatic brain injury, I was in overload mode. I was constantly exhausted.

Farm life in rural Saskatchewan was gruelling. Winter was punctuated by mice infestations and repeatedly thawing frozen pipes with propane gas torches. Then the spring thaw, water everywhere, making it impossible to keep livestock hooves dry, followed by hot summers infested with grasshoppers, grass snakes, rats, bats and mosquitoes. During storms, wind whipped the soil from adjacent land onto our property, coating every surface in the house despite windows being locked tightly shut. Overnight frosts could kill our garden produce, so I would replant everything only to have subsequent frosts make harvesting a huge challenge. One year, we suffered overnight frosts every single month of the year. Never mind trying to get hay crops off the land to feed the livestock.

But life was also exhilarating. Yes, the work was unrelenting, but there were also newborn calves, foals, puppies and kittens, and the kids and I felt their comforting love. The landscape was beautiful in the extremes of each season: with the hoarfrost and frozen water lines, sandbars in a sandstorm, sunsets with explosions of grasshoppers, I found beauty all around me, everywhere I looked.

And I felt nurtured most of all when working in my garden.

I also loved having the kids' friends over for birthday parties and big sleepovers. Everyone was always welcome. When Elsa was a teenager and alcohol was part of her partying, she and her friends often went to the fishing hole overnight and descended on the farm for breakfast. I willingly served up waffles or crepes for everyone each time. I greatly appreciate continuing to hear from many of them about how much they enjoyed those days. I doubt they enjoyed them as much as I did.

We were not serious mass-producing farmers. We treasured our animals and they all had names; my children even named each chicken. When I served beef for dinner the kids would ask, "Are we eating Cyclone tonight?" Cyclone had been a particularly mean-spirited cow, and everyone jokingly took a stab at the meat on their plate with lots of laughter. Maybe I passed on a sick sense of British humour.

One bull calf had survived a traumatic birth. His tongue lolled sideways out of his mouth for months and as a result we bottle fed him. I laughed when the children named him Frenchy. We probably should have castrated him, a steer for meat, but after becoming so closely attached we left him intact. The kids loved to bet strangers visiting the farm that they could ride the bull bareback. Frenchy loved the children as much as they loved him.

My Old English Sheepdogs became my best friends during this time. My life revolved around my children, number one, the SDWF, number two, and the farm, number three. I had no social life; one deep regret is that I let my female friendships fade because I became as obsessed as Hans to step up and do what I felt was right. My dogs filled my void for friendship; no matter how little time I gave them, they loved me unconditionally.

Once the sheepdogs started producing puppies, I developed a website and began selling them across North America.[55] I had huge disagreements with the Canadian and American Kennel clubs (CKC and AKC) and the Old English Sheepdog Club of America (OESCA), simply because they all refused to stop docking tails of this breed.

The children and a puppy "chilling" on Frenchy the bull.

Because I refused to dock the pups' tails, I was not allowed to show or register my puppies as purebreds.

I found it hard to understand why people were willing to pay more for a puppy than they were for a side of beef. They would quibble about prices for organic poultry and meat, but a soft cuddly loveable bundle of fur! They had no problem paying big money for that. I quickly learned which would earn more revenue.

Thor was a male dog with a beautiful temperament who sadly passed away from cancer at three years old and never bred any puppies. He saved my life one day. I had taken our bull to another farm to breed a friend's cows. I hauled him back home, arriving in the dark, unloaded him to the corral closest to the barn and went to bed. The next morning, I strolled around to the back door of the barn, completely forgetting I had unloaded the bull there the night before. I guess I should have had my morning coffee first. I woke up with a start; the bull was hoofing the ground and snorting and began to charge me. Thor was by my side, thank goodness; the dog immediately jumped in front of me and flew onto the bull's head, distracting him for a few seconds and giving me time to move to the

For years my world revolved around family and the politics of the SDWF, but my Sheepdog puppies were a welcome distraction.

side door of the barn and escape. I could not have been more thankful. We were all heartbroken when we lost him to cancer.

I gradually grew my puppy business. I tracked my puppies who went to homes all over North America. Sven and Elsa were great at helping when the puppies were born and until they left home at eight weeks. It was hard work, but it was happy and rewarding. At my peak, I had thirteen Old English Sheepdogs, all of which I had to train well, as they all came in the house, and all the puppies were always born indoors. I had two litters born on Christmas Eve 2006, and two litters born on Boxing Day. There were forty-six puppies in the house for New Year's Eve. Since each bitch only has eight teats, I had to rotate pups hourly, making sure the runts got more than their share against the brutes of each litter. Adam came home that Christmas and cooked a wonderful dinner for us all, and I was so grateful.

Adam gifted me a magnetic notebook for the fridge for Christmas. It had dalmatians all around the border, with a quote saying, "No one can have too many dogs." He wrote on the first page, "No one has never lived here."

That was when I decided I needed to cut back my breeding. It was a bittersweet decision, as the puppies had helped to make ends meet for many years.

12

Water on Fire

Our home phone continued to ring from five in the morning until midnight each day. So many First Nations communities wanted help, and many had terrible stories to share. There were stillbirths, miscarriages, heart attacks and cancers. I listened to repeated stories about people who required dialysis and had to travel hundreds of kilometres for treatment. I found myself questioning: How come so many First Nation individuals required kidney dialysis? While it seemed obvious to me that there could be adverse patient outcomes if the dialysis was conducted with unsafe water, it is vital to ensure the water used to perform dialysis is safe and clean. I also wondered if kidney failure could be a response to drinking unsafe water. I can't help but question why so many First Nation people developed kidney failure: Could it be attributed to the unsafe drinking water? The lack of safe drinking water was due to ineffective treatment plants that had never measured up. The list of issues grew each day, and I had enormous compassion, which transferred to my personal drive to find donors to help them all.

One day, Hans and I were driving along the Highway 1 West. We planned to hang a right and take Highway 2 North toward home. I was driving, as I always did whenever Hans and I travelled together. Hans was always needing to review a scientific paper, provide comments to a PhD student or simply read one of his heavy hardcover science books. The black leather "bag phone," as we called it, was sitting below the gear shift. It was too large to sit in the gap between our two bucket seats. It was one of the first cell phones, fixed in place in the bag, which was the size of a shoebox. When we unzipped the lid, we could pull out an extending antenna. By lifting the bag and holding it on the dashboard, if we were lucky enough to be in a hot spot, we could pick up or make phone calls, holding the receiver to our ears, much like the old telephones of days gone by.

Hans was talking on the phone, and as he hung up, he declared, "Perfect timing. We're not going straight home, head to Jim's, he wants to show me some farmers nearby who have problems with their water."

And so, we continued west on Highway 1 to Rush Lake. It was already late in the day, and I was tired. It was early springtime, and while the city streets and sidewalks were almost clear of snow, rural gravel roads still had their three distinct tracks. If I met anyone coming toward us, one of us had to jump tracks and make a new trail.

As we approached Jim's farmyard, I noted that they still had the remains of their snow pile, where the children had tobogganed most of the winter. Although the dirty grey mounds were still evident, the melting snow was adding to the runoff, leaving large puddles of water everywhere around the yard, often with twigs or hay floating in them. Farm dogs had begun shedding their winter coats, and they looked as dirty as the water pooled around them. The dogs greeted us noisily.

The farmhouse door opened before we could get out of the car. "We put the coffee on, thanks so much for coming by."

I knew the rules: Don't ever accept a coffee or anything made with water from any of these farms. It wasn't hard for me, as I had stopped drinking coffee decades ago. Rice Krispie cakes were on a plate to welcome us, and I felt the middle-aged couple were ready to give us their firstborn in appreciation for us stopping by, they were so grateful.

As always, Hans took samples of their water, a sample from each tap in the house. You could have heated up a cup of their water and anyone would have thought it was tea. Each sample looked just like the puddles of water outside.

Each farm we visited that night made us feel welcomed. Although we were strangers when we arrived, I felt like we were saying goodbye to old friends when we left. Each of the farmers had disgusting brown water, and one young family complained they couldn't bathe their children in it, so once a week they drove to Swift Current to take them to a swimming pool to get showered. I felt ill at the thought of these poor people needing to boil and then drink this awful water. More than one family lifted their T-shirts to show us the open sores on their bodies. The stories were always similar: they were on wells and septic fields and had no one but themselves to solve the problems, and no money to invest into any fancy purification systems. Reverse osmosis wasn't the answer, as the number of dissolved organics, or floaties, in the water was so high it would have clogged any reverse osmosis membrane within minutes.

One of the farms we visited that night etched a place in my heart that will never heal. The farmer claimed his drinking water could light a match. *Impossible*, I thought to myself. I would still say it was impossible today if I hadn't seen it with my own eyes.

They kept a box of matches on the counter, ready to light the propane stove. I looked at the old stainless-steel sink and it reminded me of the fuel stains left on asphalt after a leaky vehicle had parked there. The farmer ran the tap and we watched a murky, brownish water pour into the stained sink. Then, he reached for the round, dark brown switch on the old farmhouse kitchen wall and flicked off the light. We stood in darkness, waiting. He took a single match from the box and held it close to the water, probably the width of one finger away from the cascading water and halfway between the tap and the sink. Suddenly, the match caught light; there was sufficient gas streaming from the tap to ignite the match without striking. A ball of fire erupted and continued burning until he dropped the red-hot remnants of the match into the sink.

I was in shock. Hans was not, as he had seen it before on many reserves. This was the first time he saw it in a white person's rural home. The farmer flicked the kitchen light back on, and I think he saw my look of utter amazement. The drinking water was likely contaminated

The farmers' drinking water resembled the muddy spring puddles in their fields.

with methane, which has a high solubility in water.[56]

The farmer had tried to get help from a provincial authority with no success. They had claimed he must have his manure pile too close to his wellhead, that methane gas must be the culprit, that it must be leaching into his well. He was adamant that was not the case. This was typical of the problems in rural areas. It seemed to me to be a never-ending circle. Just as I listened to all the horror stories from First Nations about their terrible medical conditions resulting from their contaminated drinking water, so too did I listen to repeated stories of farmers trying to alert or request support from government agencies. When they explained their contaminated drinking water concerns, the government departments responsible pulled excuse number nineteen, or perhaps number thirteen, from a hat and blamed it on the farmer, or justified it as being naturally occurring. I never once heard of any government agency giving a reasonable response. I never heard of anyone willing to support individual farmers and their water problems. I have a feeling this was one of so many that Hans was not able to help.

There is controversy as to whether major increases in methane is a naturally occurring phenomenon or if it could be the result of fracking. However, research indicates we can no longer blame the cows for the amount of methane entering the atmosphere as the main contributors to greenhouse gasses. Fracking has been identified as taking first place: "We know the increase is largely due to fossil fuel production and this research suggests over half is from shale gas operations," says Robert Howarth, an ecologist at Cornell

University.[57] I would like to see an inquiry, treated as a research project, whereby a map showing the fracking seams beneath the earth has an overlay showing all the places where methane is detectable in the drinking water.

Eventually, Hans and I climbed back into the car and headed north, then west. I felt great relief when I reached Beechy and Elbow; I was familiar with this area from all the 4H horse shows we had attended. For a short period of time I could park my obsessive thoughts about farmers and their drinking water. I needed to feed my soul—the unending work for the SDWF overwhelmed and controlled each day of my life. I stepped back into my world of my family, and my mind drifted back to the previous summer when I had taken Sven and Elsa to a 4H horse show in Central Butte. Debbie Joel was our 4H leader and one of the kindest, most generous and honourable women I have ever met. She invited us to board our horses overnight at her friend's farm nearby. After we unloaded the horses in her friend's corral, I offered to pay her for their feed and overnight stay.

Her friend simply replied, "No need, just pay it forward."

To which Sven responded, "If you knew my mum, you wouldn't have said that."

Hans and I arrived home, exhausted, in the early hours of the morning.

✠

For the first few years with SDWF, we presumed most politicians didn't know what was happening in First Nations and rural communities. I co-ordinated many letter-writing campaigns, writing to federal politicians, asking them to act. It became obvious quickly that they all knew the problems only too well. It also became clear that most politicians wanted to sweep safe drinking water issues under any carpet they could find.

In one of my letter-writing campaigns to all members of parliament (MPs), I suggested that they vote in favour of the United Nations' declaration that safe drinking water is a basic human right.

Why did Canada, among other developed countries, abstain from voting to recognize the resolution? Only one MP, Peter McKay, replied. He explained he would not sign the declaration in case the United States put demands on Canada for access to our source waters when states like Nevada were "dry." At least he responded.

During other letter campaigns, a handful of dedicated MPs followed up and tried to push our mission forward, but little was achieved. I do believe that many people enter the political arena wanting to do the best for their constituents, but too often their hands are tied, just as Hans was bound and gagged at the SRC. MPs such as Nathan Cullen, Jon Gerrard and Charlie Angus made sincere efforts to improve conditions in Indigenous communities. Jack Layton was also a strong supporter of the SDWF.

I first met Elizabeth May in person around 1999, when I attended a reading for her book, *At the Cutting Edge: The Crisis in Canada's Forests*, at McNally Robinson in Saskatoon. After the crowd dispersed, I approached her and shared my thoughts, that if she had substituted the word "water" for "trees" throughout her book, then we could write a second book. The injustices were so similar.

Our paths crossed many times after that. I learned how, in the 1970s, May advocated for environmental issues, gaining particular attention for her attempts to stop the spraying of pesticides over forests in Nova Scotia. And in 2001, while serving as executive director of the Sierra Club of Canada, May staged a seventeen-day hunger strike to draw attention to the Sydney Tar Ponds, an industrial waste site responsible for illnesses and birth defects in the former city of Sydney (now part of the Cape Breton regional municipality) and the surrounding area. I wonder at how similar the issues facing communities downstream of the tar sands in Alberta are.

Politicians weren't the only ones who didn't want to know about the plight of First Nations' and rural Canadians' drinking water: conventional national and provincial media often showed zero interest in exposing the issues, no matter how hard I tried. The CBC occasionally picked up on one of our releases and did a story, and they often called Hans to get his perspective on a water-related issue

In the truck with the boxes of letters addressed to members of parliament.

in the news. A highlight was when CBC's Bob McDonald, host of *Quirks & Quarks*, came to Yellow Quill to film and air a documentary on Hans's work there. But when we tried to raise funds and awareness, our media releases and other efforts mostly fell on deaf ears. Warren Goulding alludes to this problem in his book *Just Another Indian*:

> The mainstream media, as both a mirror of society's values and the messenger that delivers the dispatches it senses the public is keen to receive, make a judgment based on what they deem important and worthy of space or airtime. The writers and editors working there bring an inherent prejudice to the workplace, much of it rooted in ignorance. It doesn't help that there are few aboriginal journalists employed in Canadian newsrooms.[58]

It would be wrong of me to portray media as disinterested in *First Nations'* drinking water; they appeared to be disinterested in *any* drinking water issue. I was always so thankful to all the independent publications, like the *Rural Councillor* or *Canada Water Treatment,* who did their best to inform and educate their readers on drinking water issues.

We continued to establish trust between the SDWF and First Nations leaders and work closely with leaders to help them assert their right for safe drinking water from INAC. Hans was instrumental in this, working with First Nations water operators, chiefs and councillors and continuing to stand up for them. He provided wordsmithing and implemented documents, enabling leaders to take back control, often passing bylaws for their community, which could only pass with INAC's approval. He patiently explained the science in everyday language they (and I) could understand. His daily encouragement helped operators to reach their potential, regaining pride and ownership. They became empowered to stand up for themselves when dealing with the federal bureaucracy.

13

Hans Brings the SDWF
to the United Nations

Tom BK Goldtooth, the executive director of Indigenous Environmental Network and the individual who opened our 2004 conference, invited Hans to speak about Yellow Quill First Nations at the United Nations headquarters in New York on April 19, 2005. Hans took Roberta Neapetung, the young woman he had trained as a water treatment operator, and they gave the presentation together.

The Indigenous Environmental Network wanted to share stories of success when it came to safe drinking water conditions in Indigenous communities and, as Hans writes, they "ended up choosing Yellow Quill to represent a community's successful struggle for safe drinking water, even if it did take nine years."[59] Hans was able to share with the world how the Yellow Quill Water Treatment Plant

> meets both national [guidelines] and international regulations for safe drinking water and Yellow Quill is indeed bottling some water from the plant. There were many innovations at the Yellow Quill's water treatment plant and the engineering company responsible for scale-up received two awards of engineering excellence for the project.[60]

Hans and Roberta's presentation opened doors for funding and opened eyes globally to the situation in First Nations communities. There was also hope at the time that the presentation would mark the beginning of organizing an Aboriginal R&D Water Treatment Centre in an area of Saskatchewan where the source water is poor and salty.[61]

All the same, I continued to receive requests from First Nations communities asking for help with their drinking water problems every day. One nation in Northern Ontario called with the same health issues I had heard of so many times, issues they were certain to be caused by their poor water: infant mortality, stillbirths, kidney failure and serious skin problems. This community had insisted on Health Canada testing their water and were repeatedly told it was safe, that their water met all guidelines for Canadian Drinking Water Quality. And it was not just one round of testing; many tests came back, and Health Canada said the same thing: "Nothing is wrong."

I asked them to send copies of their most recent analyses for Hans to review. When Hans read the reports, he was furious. This was a remote community in Northern Ontario surrounded by lakes and natural habitat affected by the diamond mines in operation nearby. Yet, Health Canada had run standard water analyses that were suitable for the prairies, looking for pesticides and heavy metals associated with spring runoff from agriculture. They did not conduct analysis for either mercury or lead in the community drinking water, which were the principal causes of their health issues. This was a lightbulb moment for me. Now I understood why EJLB pulled their sponsorship when we first founded the SDWF. They were fine with us helping developing countries, and they probably recognized it would only be a matter of time until we uncovered the issues affecting First Nations communities that were caused by diamond mining. The EJLB was funded in large part by De Beers at the time of their donation.

Hans took up the critical error in the testing with both the heads of INAC and Health Canada. Health Canada responded to the community leaders acknowledging that they had made an error, and Hans wondered whether they were incompetent or ashamed to have been caught. When we conducted testing of the source and treated water, it was obvious the treatment system was inadequate, a system that was clearly constructed according to the "Low-Cost Rule." This was a pattern across the country, one that has resulted in

> poor quality engineering, poor quality workman-
> ship, poor quality equipment, and poor-quality
> treated water. More than 90 percent of Canada's
> First Nations' water treatment plants cannot meet
> the full complement of the Guidelines for Canadian
> Drinking Water Quality... As long as the Low-Cost
> Rule is the rule that is followed, ... First Nations
> are bound to just get more of the same. Bad tasting
> and unsafe tap water, ... water so bad that it results
> in sores on community members' bodies, some-
> thing not even expected in a Third World city and
> country like Kampala, Uganda, even if the water is
> undrinkable there. If INAC has a fiduciary respon-
> sibility toward First Nations, it cannot discharge
> all its responsibilities simply by looking at only the
> lowest bid. What good is a water treatment plant if
> the product coming out of it is toxic?[62]

In March of 2005, Attawapiskat First Nation deputy Chief Theresa Spence was trying to draw attention to the plight of her community. In the wee hours of the morning, community members noticed a rank smell inside their homes: a sewage backup had flooded the basement floors of several homes. Ontario First Nations Technical Services determined that the diamond company De Beers, which operated a mine ninety kilometres from the Attawapiskat First Nation, had dumped their sewage sludge into the First Nation's lift station.[63]

The memo (see Appendix One) was written by Ontario First Nations Technical Services and, in my opinion, placed the responsibility of this incident on the wrong party.[64] While the memo acknowledges that De Beers discharged a load of sewage into the pumping station and that this "might have precipitated the overloading of the pumping station," it also blames the community for not having a sewer-connection plumbing standard or bylaw. Would a bylaw have stopped the problem, especially if their treatment system is "very fragile and at high risk of failing"?[65] INAC oversaw and approved every bylaw any Indigenous community designed, so shouldn't it be INAC's responsibility to ensure such a bylaw is in place?

De Beers should have been held responsible for all repairs and costs associated with repairing the flooded homes and temporarily relocating the residents. The amount De Beers can dump in the future should also have been limited. Instead, the report suggested that INAC should fund a "sewer servicing study," which would have injected more money into engineers capable of producing the document, with more money going into the pockets of rich white males, instead of supporting the victims. I use this analogy because in all my time helping with the SDWF I never met a female engineer, nor a poor engineer, nor an engineer from a marginalized race or ethnicity.

The Hookimaw household listed in the memo was uninhabitable after the sewage backup. When the house was boarded up, the pipes froze and burst. The water from this incident eventually caused toxic mould to proliferate throughout the home. The Hookimaw family received a $25,000 insurance cheque. When *APTN National News* contacted De Beers, Tom Ormsby, the company's spokesman, said, "I'm sorry, I'm not familiar with the story you're talking about."[66]

I am well aware that some readers will dismiss this issue based on claims of corruption within Attawapiskat leadership. I have witnessed plenty of corruption from our own government officials in how they treat, or rather mistreat, First Nations people. In my mind, no one should be exempt from being held accountable for their behaviour. It is about changing our ways. It is an act of humanity.

14

Critique and Consequence

Hans was a prolific writer, and he often wrote scathing articles. By early 2005, he was publishing weekly. In May of that year, he published an internal briefing note to Environment Minister Stéphane Dion that was obtained through an Access to Information request. The note states that "our failure to protect water has caught up with us. Diseases from contaminated water cost our health system $300 million a year. Between 20–40 percent of rural wells are more contaminated than drinking water guidelines recommend."[67] One more example, in my opinion, of politicians knowing what was wrong, knowing how terribly First Nations people were suffering, and also how rural Canadians were not faring much better than First Nations, yet still not taking action. As Hans writes, "scientists working on water inside and outside of the federal government have known this for years."[68]

He was still actively blowing the whistle on INAC, which did not require that all treated water meets all the national guidelines on safe drinking water:

> Instead, INAC relies on Health Canada's bare bones assessments of drinking water safety (10 [percent] of the total guidelines) total and free chlorine, Escherichia coli, coliforms and nitrate. To meet four of these five parameters, water treatment plants are not necessary, only chlorine is. While Health Canada every two years or so makes more extensive analyses, these are generally not

used by INAC to assess treatment plant efficiencies
and, indeed, this information is not always communicated to INAC.[69]

In June of 2005, he published "Due Diligence Equals Safe
Drinking Water" with the *Aboriginal Times*. Due diligence, Hans
reminded his readers, means that if you know something is wrong
and if you do not reasonably try to act, you can be held liable. He
then suggested that federal departments were not practising due
diligence when it came to safe drinking water on reserves, providing the Saddle Lake Cree Nation and Six Nations of the Grand River
as examples.

Within ten days of publication, Hans received notice that the
SDWF and WRC were being evicted from the National Hydrology
Research Institute, where we had rented space for nearly a decade.
The institute gave us no reason for the eviction. We had ten days to
vacate. I was given the job of finding space to move the SDWF. Hans
decided WRC would operate from the lab we had built on the farm.

Searching for commercial real estate that a charity could afford was a huge challenge. I found a place on Idylwyld Drive North,
in Saskatoon, where SDWF still operates today. The basement location was in a decrepit state. I hired our daughter's friends to help
paint the space. We painted, scrubbed and polished for a few days,
then moved everything in.

The Canada Revenue Agency (CRA) launched an audit of the
SDWF soon after the eviction. I maintained the financial records
for the charity, and an accounting company provided the official financial statements. I posted the audited financial statements online
each year for total transparency. We were proud of our low operating costs in relation to our contribution to education. The four-
month interrogation yielded no discrepancies in our records. It did
consume too many hours of my time, taking me away from far more
rewarding tasks, and it created enormous stress.

One month later, I received notice that CRA was auditing
WRC. By now I had learned the routine. I kept the books and had
the same accounting company prepare the financial documents, as

I had done with the SDWF. A few months passed, and once again CRA found no discrepancies. Then another audit was requested, this time of the farm. After more time spent with auditors, they determined I should have charged GST on the Old English Sheepdog puppies I sold. We rectified that error by paying the amount due, but CRA was still not content. They then audited both Hans's and my personal returns. The audits spanned more than three years and required hundreds of hours of my time. The entire experience was stressful and incurred significant costs to taxpayers. I inevitably felt the audits were not coincidental, that they were payback for the article Hans published on due diligence. Pressure was mounting, and they were trying to shut him up.

As a gesture of appreciation, the Chief and Council of Yellow Quill gave Hans a wig of Indigenous braids and an honourary Indian status card. It was funny, given with sincere appreciation. Everyone knew the gesture was a joke; a blue-eyed, bald man with a Swedish accent, although he was wearing his braids in the photo they took on this day of recognition, with a status card! He treasured the card as much as he did the quilts, eagle feathers and sweetgrass they had also given him.

I answered a phone call from a lawyer representing INAC a week after the appreciation celebration. He gave me five days to return the status card. He explained that it had been illegally produced, and that if I didn't return it immediately, we would be charged with fraud under the Criminal Code. I was shocked. I tried to explain, but he wouldn't listen.

I wondered what right the government had to micromanage First Nations leaders, and what the difference was for a person to receive an honourary degree from a university or an honourary status card. I couldn't comprehend how INAC responded so quickly and harshly with their legal team over an honourary status card given as a joke, yet they consistently failed to respond to the facts of ineffective water treatment systems. Why wouldn't they put lawyers in charge of all the ineffective water treatment plants they had funded? This is an example of how INAC micromanaged every First Nations council when they chose to.

I called a graphic artist friend to help me, and in less than an hour we made a duplicate mock-up of the threatened status card, and I sent it to the lawyer to alleviate his threats. Hans carried the original in his wallet until the day he died.

15

The Lives at Risk Downstream

First Nations leaders were sharing more stories of poor health among their members. Stillbirths, infant mortality, kidney disease, heart problems and many cancers were common. The more phone calls I received from Indigenous leaders, the greater my empathy for them and their struggles. While I had experienced so many years of isolation and solitude, the more I heard of their plight, the more accepting I became with my own life—although I was so lonely.

When possible, I drove to meet with leaders to determine if and how we could help them. One time when I visited Hans at Saddle Lake, I made a trip to meet with many First Nations community leaders in North Central Alberta, including those at Slave Lake, Frog Lake, Dene Tha', Beaver and Driftpile First Nation. When I visited with leaders, we often sat with cups of blueberry tea warming our hands (I knew only too well the risks I was taking, but I trusted they had boiled their water, and I could never have refused their generous hospitality). We would spend hours chatting like dear friends. Some of the communities had recently received indoor plumbing, no doubt funded by INAC, and the women wondered if perhaps the plumbing was sent almost as a bribe: see, we are giving you things, be thankful, stop complaining and asking for more. The women held painful feelings deep inside their souls. They felt like second-class citizens. Their heartache was evident in each word they uttered; I felt their pain in every syllable. I believed every word. Once I understood and witnessed the challenges, I shared their pain, their frustrations. I was angry at those in places of power for their inaction.

I felt that white people had betrayed Indigenous Peoples, that they had taken advantage of them and benefitted from their adversity. I was walking in their moccasins for a short while, but I had the option to step back into my own shoes and act is if nothing was wrong. I knew I couldn't live with myself if I joined the white attitude of denial. Now I knew, and the more I knew the more compelled I was to act, to do my best to right each wrong.

The leaders at Driftpile Cree Nation believed that the Swan Hills Treatment Centre was the cause of their concerns. They called the plant the Swan Hills Toxic Waste Dump. At the first mention of "Swan Hills," I conjured up memories in my mind of an idyllic British pond at Theydon Bois, a village near where I lived as a young girl. The image of the pond I had in mind was in springtime, and swans were swimming gracefully around, their cygnets following in their wake. I knew from experience that swans could become aggressive and protective.

After listening to the concerns of the leaders, I drove to the Swan Hills Treatment Centre to check things out. The town of Swan Hills is at an elevation of 1,113 metres, but Driftpile Cree Nation is at an elevation of 577 metres. The winding gravel road, which more resembled a logging road, took me up a small mountain. Tall evergreens stood like knights on each side of me. The Swan Hills are foothills of the Rocky Mountains, the only foothills that extend into the centre of Alberta. As I rounded the last bend, a gravel parking lot opened into my view, with room to turn around. A high chain-link fence was surrounding the compound. It was completely inaccessible; the huge, heavy chain-link gates were double padlocked. This was all I would see of the treatment facility.

I thought back to the name, Swan Hills, and I remembered the aggressive swans from my childhood. I wondered aloud, not that anyone could hear me, "Has this place been named Swan Hills to suggest a place of tranquility? Or was the name selected as they need an aggressive protector?" I had no idea where the name originated, that it was first given to the area by the local Indigenous people, who believed that giant swans nested on the estuary of the

Assiniboine river. During the summer prairie thunderstorms, it was said the thundering wing beat of these great birds filled the air as they fled for shelter.[70] Swans will fight to the bitter end. I decided the name fulfilled both purposes, the image of tranquility and protection.

Even though I didn't get to see the centre, my first thought was so logical, it did not require a scientist or engineer. No matter what was done to treat the waste, any residue disposed of on the mountaintop had to run downhill. Who were the brains behind such an endeavour? Any communities at a lower elevation had to experience the terrible consequences of this runoff.

Indeed, the plant was hit with a $625,000 fine for "leaking toxic PCBs, dioxins and furans into the atmosphere" in 1996. This was the province's largest fine ever issued for environmental violations at the time. And three years after my visit to the centre, a report would claim that the plant's landfill had begun to threaten groundwater. The report suggests that the cost of the clean-up would be $71 million. The plant would continue to cost taxpayers tens of millions of dollars in operating losses over the years. And many, if not all, of the affected communities downstream Swan Hills are still waiting for improved water treatment plants. Then premier of Alberta, Ralph Klein, expected the plant to be profitable and was willing to take responsibility for the financial failure. "But," the *Calgary Herald* quotes him saying, "I will stand behind the statement that this was not an absolute, total boondoggle."[71]

Of course, concerns from those living downstream, downwind or near the Alberta tar sands have also been significant since the 1970s. Traditional Knowledge Keepers, academics and scientists have been clear about the risk of downstream contamination. The Northern River Basin Study in 1996 "strongly recommended" a health study, and the Alberta Cancer Board Fort Chipewyan in 2009 called for the same thing. Yet "industry and the Alberta government's reactions have obstructed" the possibility; as of 2023, no study of this nature has been done, yet there are documented rare cancers in the Fort Chipewyan and Fort McMurray areas.[72]

On February 4, 2023, Imperial Oil's tailings pond leaked 5.3 million litres of toxic tailings into the environment. That same day, a second leak was reported at the same facility that had been leaking since May. As Jesse Cardinal and Paul Belanger of the Keepers of the Water organization write, the "last people notified of the tailings spills were nearby Indigenous communities of Mikisew [First Nation], Athabasca Chipewyan [First Nation] and Fort McKay [First Nation]."[73] Cardinal claims that these "impacts are felt immensely in downstream Indigenous communities and continues to perpetuate the ongoing genocide of Indigenous Peoples and yet it's become common for Indigenous communities to be the last to be informed." As of March 2023, the tar sands tailings ponds, which span an area two times the size of the city of Vancouver, contain over 1.4 trillion litres of toxic waste and include dangerous levels of mercury, arsenic and naphthenic acids.[74]

Yet the tailing ponds pose a risk whether there are spills or not. Paul Belanger, science advisor for the Keepers of the Water organization, claims that the ponds' design, approved by the Alberta Energy Regulator, does not require a liner, which increases the risk of liquids seeping into the area around the ponds and into the groundwater beneath them. Once the tailings escape, they will run through multiple watersheds before ending up in the Arctic Ocean.[75] According to Belanger, recent reports have identified toxins and harmful gases from the tailings ponds in the Athabasca watershed.[76] Furthermore:

> Canada has not obtained the Free, Prior and Informed Consent of downstream Indigenous communities. This legal requirement stems from Canada's United Nations Declaration on the Rights of Indigenous Peoples (UNDRIP) Act, which came into force in 2021. UNDRIP guarantees Indigenous Peoples the opportunity to participate in state legislative and policy initiatives that directly and negatively impact the watershed they live in and rely on for sustenance.[77]

I agree with Belanger: the least the government could do is ensure downstream communities have effective water treatment systems. But the "tragic lack of regulatory action and the complicit behaviour by both industry and the Alberta government [have] turned the entire oil sand area into a sacrificial zone. It is a large-scale example of environmental racism."[78]

Too many Canadians, often white affluent males, be they owners of "Big Oil" or engineering companies or the CEOs of banks, stand to benefit disproportionally to others who are negatively impacted by their decisions. The annual Banking on Climate Chaos report shows that the Royal Bank of Canada's (RBC's) funding between 2016 and 2021 put it as the fifth-largest fossil fuel funder, and a report from a coalition of environmental groups shows that it was the biggest fossil fuel financier in the world in 2022 after providing over $42 billion USD in funding.[79] Compare that to the paycheque of RBC's CEO David McKay, who had the largest paycheque of bank CEOs in Canada in 2021, receiving $15.5 million in direct compensation, a 25 percent increase from the previous year. In addition to his base salary of $1.5 million, McKay received more than $4 million in short-term incentives based on the bank meeting financial, client, risk and strategic objectives. McKay's short-term incentive award was 82 percent above target. The rest of McKay's compensation came from performance deferred share units and stock options totalling almost $10 million.[80]

I would like to see a comparison of the total of RBC philanthropic donations to McKay's salary. I see rewards such as this as criminal when those affected are living in squalor and abject poverty and without safe drinking water. What right does anyone have to huge profits benefitted from the ongoing abuse of Indigenous Peoples? At a bare minimum, Big Oil should be providing effective water treatment systems that meet or exceed WHO water quality guidelines to all communities impacted by their operations. If we step outside the parameters of my focus on safe drinking water and consider the implications on climate change, these figures seem even more abhorrent to me.

Privilege, as Shaun Loney argues in *The Beautiful Bailout,* always comes at the cost of the poverty of someone else.[81] Andrew Nikiforuk says something similar in *The Energy of Slaves*:

> Today, many people in industrialized countries enjoy lifestyles as extravagant as those of Caribbean plantation owners. We feel entitled to surplus energy and rationalise inequality, even barbarity to get it. But endless growth depends on cheap energy, and our primary slave fuels are getting more expensive by the day. What we need... is a radical new emancipation movement that confronts the most pressing challenge we face: learning to use energy on a moral and truly human scale.[82]

Of course, there's a sickness at the heart of the system. As economist Milton Friedman claims, "a corporation is the property of its stockbrokers. ... [S]hould it spend the stockbroker's money for purposes which it regards as socially responsible but which it cannot connect to its bottom line? The answer I would say is no."[83]

In 2010, there was public outrage at the euthanasia of 230 ducks that landed in the Mildred Lake tailings pond and made contact with the toxic by-products. This came a few days after Syncrude, one of the world's largest producers of synthetic crude oil, agreed to a $3-million penalty for the death of 1,600 ducks in a different tailings pond in April 2008. The ducks were euthanized according to the advice of Alberta fish and wildlife officials. Of the incident, Environment Minister Rob Renner said, "I cannot express how disappointed and frustrated I am that this incident occurred. Albertans deserve answers to why this happened again, and we will do everything we can to get those answers quickly."[84]

But why are ducks more important than Indigenous lives? It reminds me of how tobacco companies knew for decades that cigarettes negatively impacted people's health, yet they continued to market their toxic product to customers, especially attempting to hook young people. In the same way, the oil companies and the government know exactly how they are affecting the health of the members of the Fort McKay, Athabasca Chipewyan, Mikisew Cree, Chipewyan Prairie, Fort McMurray First Nations and the Métis communities in Northern Alberta. And, of course, these oil sands operate on stolen land.[85]

16

Priorities

Whitecap Dakota First Nation, located close to our farm on Highway 219, opened a casino in 2007 following years of controversial public debates. Hundreds of people were attracted daily to gamble their luck, yet no Saskatchewan government department was concerned that the area was plagued with poor water quality. Soon after the casino opened, the million-dollar aesthetic waterfall they had built in the Vegas-style entrance became clogged. The waterfall was no longer falling! Call in Dr. Hans, or "DR H2O," as his vehicle's licence plate read: they needed a water treatment plant to ensure the waterfall kept working. It was magical how quickly INAC approved funding for the casino's IBROM water treatment plant. Thanks to Chief Darcy Bear, it was soon followed by another IBROM water treatment plant that provided safe drinking water to the entire Whitecap community.

The public has often been told about hundreds of thousands of dollars being thrown at First Nations, as if these communities' benefit from the funding. All too often they don't. It is another way of siphoning money to engineers, corporations or government consultants—individuals who are often white, often male, often already wealthy. For example, when Health Canada received more than $150 million to address safe drinking water in First Nations communities across the country, it simply increased their coliform testing to once per week instead of once per month.[86] Do you think this money benefitted First Nations people?

Take another example: in 2005, the Kashechewan First Nation's drinking water became contaminated with E. coli. Although the community had a new treatment plant installed ten years prior to replace the dilapidated one, many expressed concern that it was too small to manage the growing community. When E. coli levels spiked dangerously in 2005, the amount of chlorine increased to "shock levels," ongoing skin problems such as scabies and impetigo worsened and a quarter of the residents were evacuated by plane—a procedure that is estimated to have cost $16 million.[87] As usual, the federal and provincial governments and Health Canada labelled this a "one-time disaster," giving no consideration to the pre-existing presence of chronic skin issues; the Kashechewan First Nation declared it an "ongoing crisis."[88]

"Feeling guilty or shamed into taking some sort of action..., the federal government, with little to lose from making lofty promises," Hans writes, "did it in grand style by stating that fifty new houses will be built per year for the next decade." This is a good thing as the housing needs in Kashechewan are significant. "[But] I have to question the federal government's action of putting in the housing, complete with water and sewer pipes connected to the dwelling, which I suspect may deliver questionable water quality to the new inhabitants?" Confusing, to say the least.[89]

From my time spent in various First Nations communities, I repeatedly saw housing that was built like packs of cards. A huff and a puff and they would come tumbling down. Like water treatment facilities, housing also was built according to the low-cost bid. It is baffling that the feds would barter new houses in place of building an effective water treatment plant. This bartering tells me two things: it was the cheaper option and a blatant misuse of taxpayer money.

My opinion was validated when I read this passage from Warren Goulding's *Just Another Indian*. In the Peigan reserve,

> the homes are sited far apart. Most could benefit
> from a visit from a battery of skilled tradespeople.
> Shoddy workmanship and inferior materials com-
> bined with the relentless onslaught of the wind,

and in some cases, neglect and abuse, have caused many of the homes to fall into disrepair. If not for the fact that they were located in an Indian reserve, many would long ago have been declared uninhabitable.[90]

Why don't we provide funding so First Nations can build their own houses? The only answer I can envisage is that it would take money away from colonial beneficiaries.

I can't help but wonder if this is a modern case of the smallpox-infested blankets the colonizers distributed to First Nations communities in the mid-eighteenth century. I feel guilty for thinking these accusatory thoughts, but then I recall Darrel McLeod's memoir *Mamaskatch*, where he made similar comparisons.

> I wouldn't understand it until years later, when I read about the massacre of the buffalo: reduced from thirty million to around three hundred in eighty years. It was part of a bigger government plan to force the Plains Cree into submission; starve them. Bad medicine.[91]

I need not feel any guilt for raising this possibility when the facts speak for themselves. While there are some who insist the smallpox blankets were a myth, I believe the stories handed down over generations in Indigenous communities, just as I believed each story of children dying in residential schools before the graves were identified.

17

Pervasive Ignorance

In 2007, I believe I made a few good decisions for the success of the SDWF, but my best decision was probably to hire Nicole Biederbeck, now Nicole Hancock. Funds were limited; I could only offer her part-time employment. She also worked as an instructor at a learning centre and for a non-profit federation and was happy with the arrangement to work with us when needed. She embraced the flexibility and became as enthusiastic as both Hans and me, striving for perfection in all her tasks. I am thrilled that seventeen years later, she remains a constant figure in the organization and her passion and dedication continue to drive the SDWF in her role as executive director.

One morning, Nicole and I arrived at the SDWF office to an email informing us that the SDWF website had been linked to a marketing ploy by Mott's Clamato juice. We checked Mott's website where they posed the question, "Do you think Mott's Clamato Juice is sexy?" If you clicked "yes," you were directed to a coupon for free Mott's products. If you clicked "no," you were sent to the SDWF website.

I sent emails to Mott's with no response. I had a lawyer send letters stating it was inappropriate, asking that the website link be removed and suggesting that SDWF should be compensated. Some people may ask, "Why was it inappropriate? It would drive traffic to the SDWF website, and all it means about those people is they do not think Mott's Clamato juice is sexy."

I previously attended a function with Hans where I sat beside an MLA, and Hans seized the opportunity to talk to her about the plight of Indigenous Peoples and their drinking water. She quickly excused herself and said, "This is so boring, I am going to join the conversation on the other side of me, their topic sounds much sexier!"

I found the Mott's website attack, like the MLA's response, to be a statement of disregard for what was happening, and an attempt to undermine the work of the SDWF. I found it inappropriate as the internet is a little like the Wild West, and the SDWF had not authorized the link. The website is the home of the SDWF. I compare it to strangers advising their network of friends to come to your house, and I believed it presented a negative connotation.

Mott's eventually took down the link to the SDWF after a couple of weeks, but offered no apology as they claimed that it had been done by an advertising company hired by Mott's and that Mott's had no control over the campaign.

I had become used to this type of perception, not that being used to it made it less jarring. Another time, I was with other parents preparing to chauffeur our teenagers to a rural basketball game in another community. The physical education teacher greeted us, gave us driving directions and then mockingly looked at me as he stated, "And Mrs. Peterson will decide where we stop for coffee to ensure no one gets sick from the water." Other parents laughed at his joke. It was much easier for people to mock us for our work than to understand the science—until they ended up needing our services too. More people in our home community and from other rural Saskatchewan communities also began calling for help. "My brother is concerned about the well on his farm." Everyone, it seemed, had a family member with concerns about their water. Yet these people believed they had a right to ask Hans to test their water for free!

I took one family to task. They ran a seemingly profitable business and I felt they could comfortably pay. I asked, "How would you like to provide your services to our foundation for free?" When I hung up the phone, I felt a huge awakening. So, this is entitlement. Many assume that a charity has funds to help fulfill their mission, but do they realize how hard it is to attract funding? We didn't have the resources to help everyone.

The more phone calls I received, the more funds, foundations and philanthropists I needed to find. And the more I sought help, the more dejected I felt. While some donors stepped up, and I am forever grateful to them, so many left me with a feeling that they were indifferent to the plight of First Nations people. Or at best, indifferent to any issues surrounding drinking water in Canada. I was kept awake at night making hard decisions. It was impossible to help each community in need and there were simply not enough funds, while our neighbours wanted SDWF services for free.

My experience has taught me that ignorance is the route of much suffering. Consider what Hans published in the *Prince Albert Grand Council Tribune*:

> When I was in Ottawa one time, I had a discussion with a top-level civil servant. Like someone in the twenty-first century still impressed with a fax machine when we have email and other means of instant communications, he dwelled on the simplicity and virtues of granular filtration (particle filtration) and he thought that this was the path of the future for water treatment in Canada's First Nations!! Gasp! I simply had no words for this. This is the road the federal government has taken for decades and this is the road that has got us into the current pickle with few First Nations being able to produce safe and drinkable distributed water. It is the wrong road.[92]

I am baffled by science, but even I can plainly see Hans's cynicism in this article for *Canadian Water Treatment*:

> In February 2005, the BC government launched a new $80 million safe drinking water program. There were a number of reasons for implementing this program, which included curbing boil water advisories that jumped from 19 in 1986 to 304 in 2001 and the reduction of disease-causing

water-borne microbes (pathogens) such as E. coli and Hepatitis A. It is gratifying that Hepatitis A is recognized by a provincial government agency as a cause for concern when it comes to water safety. Years ago, the US Environmental Protection Agency demonstrated that 7 percent of studied wells in that country contained the Hepatitis A virus and its presence was one of the reasons for the implementation of the US Groundwater Rule. While this was common knowledge among scientists years ago, the then chief medical health officer for Saskatchewan, Dr. Butler-Jones, proclaimed publicly that Hepatitis A was only water-borne in developing countries. It appears that with time, provincial and federal health agencies will concede defeat and stop playing politics and start using rather than abusing science.[93]

I have seen for decades, from all colours of politics, how science is ignored, buried within the bureaucracy striving to maintain or increase control or to get votes. Jody Wilson-Raybould speaks of this in her 2021 memoir *Indian in the Cabinet* about her time as a member of parliament for the Trudeau government. One of the mandate letters made public shortly after her swearing-in on November 4, 2015, was that "'science and the rule of law and the Constitution must be woven through everything we do.'" There was talk of "speaking truth to power," and Wilson-Raybould identified with that. But, as she writes in her memoir, she would find out that she was not supposed to take that claim seriously, that topics such as reconciliation can be seen as serious issues within cabinet but not taken seriously politically.[94] Wilson-Raybould's naïveté at the time reflected the false front the federal government put forward to the Canadian public. If our politicians don't mean what they say, what do they offer their electorate?

Wilson-Raybould also recalls her vivid memory of one of her first conversations with a colleague, who excitedly exclaimed that

Wilson-Raybould was the first Indigenous person they had ever met. Something like this happened to a friend of mine, who was meeting with a white woman in an attempt to bring to light the water conditions in First Nations communities. The white woman said, "I can't believe I'm talking to a real Indian! I've never met an Indian before." She was a high-ranking professional in a large corporation, with zero tact, sensitivity or cultural awareness.

During his university days, Sven was working on his political science degree and often volunteered to help Hans and the SDWF. In an article he published with James Gibson, a summer student at the SDWF, they addressed the difference between "serious issues" and what's taken "seriously politically":

> When we turn on the tap, we assume that the water has been treated properly and is safe to drink. We know that someone is responsible for ensuring the water is safe and if it causes illness, that they will be held accountable. We believe that the money spent by the government results in better drinking water. But for many First Nations communities, this simply is not the case. A major reason for this is that unlike in other communities, there are no legally enforceable regulations with clear standards and responsibilities that are monitored by an independent body.[95]

The impetus for their article was the release of the commissioner of the environment and sustainable development's report criticizing INAC and Health Canada's intervention in the safe drinking water of First Nations communities in 2005. The report claimed that despite "the hundreds of millions in federal funds invested" in safe drinking water, these communities still do not have safe tap water because no "comprehensive guidelines" means there are "significant gaps in responsibility."[96] Sven and James continue:

> In the absence of legally enforceable standards, INAC has had to develop internal protocols to

guide the treatment of drinking water in First Nations communities. Even here though, these protocols are often not followed. An internal evaluation by INAC found that less than half of First Nations communities monitored their water every week as they are required. Government agencies also do not meet the standards they themselves set. The same evaluation found that Health Canada did not test almost half of communities for trihalomethanes (THMs) quarterly and 77 percent were not tested for various other chemical contaminants annually as required. Nor did INAC annually inspect all water treatment systems as required. There have also been situations where Health Canada has refused to call for a boil water advisory despite its own guidance for when to call a boil water advisory was met (loss of chlorine residuals in the distribution system, Saddle Lake Cree Nation, AB).

Finally, there is the issue of resources. Without sufficient resources, good regulations will simply create standards that cannot be met. Until there is enough funding for adequate treatment plants, regulations will have little impact.[97]

In 2008, Chuck Strahl, the INAC Minister at the time, said that "it might make sense, ... depending on the area, to have well water and septic systems, for example, or cisterns or other ways to make sure water is potable and safe" rather than large water treatment systems.[98] Strahl thought safe drinking water was available, and it was as simple as digging a well. This thinking reflects the level of education and/or the level of understanding of politicians and key decision makers. Until scientists with strong ethical values, integrity and passion to do the right thing advise and direct the treatment processes for First Nations, we cannot rely on politicians with pathetic answers.

18

Stanley Mission

In 2007, phone calls started coming in from Stanley Mission in Northern Saskatchewan, on the Churchill River. They wanted help with their sewage treatment. The treatment plant always reeked, and the current system could not meet the demands of the community. Hans was proud that he had developed water treatment systems for both ground and surface source waters, and many communities were benefitting. Adapting the IBROM system into the first biological sewage treatment facility became Hans's number one obsession.

With this new focus, he moved to Stanley Mission, a seven-hour drive from the farm, with the last hour of the journey on winding gravel logging roads that guaranteed you would suffer a flat tire along the way. The community was unique because it was located on a peninsula. Next to the First Nations community is another community for non-Indigenous residents. Hans made many trips to Stanley Mission, and sometimes I accompanied him. On one of my first trips there, we canoed across the Churchill River to visit the Holy Trinity Anglican Church, a historical building on the banks of the river opposite the community. The church had been designed by Reverend Robert Hunt, an English missionary who founded Stanley Mission in 1851, one hundred years before I was born. The name sent shivers down my spine: my grandfather was Bert Hunt, and his older brother was named Robert, although he goes by Bob, and both the reverend named Bob Hunt and my grandfather's family came from Essex in the UK. My grandfather's youngest brother, Jack, sponsored me to immigrate to Canada, and he also named his eldest son Bob. It wasn't the first time I believed a greater power had placed me where I was meant to be.

Eventually, I found a piece of property for sale on the shores of the Churchill River and we bought it. A nearby home was deemed uninhabitable due to a diesel fire in the fuel tank outside the house, but the home itself was still intact. I coordinated the purchase and relocation of the damaged home, as well as renovations. I made sure the home was positioned on the new property in such a way as to give us a wonderful view overlooking the Churchill River through a large window. I renovated the home while Hans worked long hours to develop a wastewater treatment process.

Hans was focussed on his sewage treatment research that summer. I got to know the people in the community, including the children and teachers at the school as they taught the Operation Water Drop program. While the Churchill River is one of Canada's most beautiful natural environments, I found the isolation and limited lifestyle not to my liking. Hans, however, embraced cross-country skiing in the winter, kayaking in summer and he enjoyed the slow pace of the community.

One day, Hans ran through the Stanley Mission house shouting, "I knew it was going to happen, it was just a matter of time! Did you hear the news? Beaver Fever has hit Toronto, what I have always predicted. Now people will start to listen."

"What are you talking about?" I replied. "I haven't heard any such thing."

"Yes, yes, it's all over CBC." And with that, he began calling his media contacts, who had interviewed him in the past. None of them had any news about "beaver fever," a common name for giardiasis, in Toronto and politely told him they would call when they received notice of it.

I was driving into town the next day and listening to the news: "'Bieber Fever' has gripped the city of Toronto. Fans thronged together at the airport to welcome Justin Bieber home." I began to laugh hysterically. Anyone driving alongside me must have thought

I was nuts. There it was: "Beaver Fever." It was never talked about again.

We were to celebrate my fifty-ninth birthday at Stanley Mission with our friend Marvin, along with his wife, their daughter and her boyfriend. Marvin had completed many carpenter projects for us over the years and had become a good friend. NBTB Woodwork, Nothing But The Best, and he lived up to his name. He and his wife pioneered the first tiny home I ever saw, quite a masterpiece of space.

I had brought with me food for a nice barbeque, and Marvin and family had driven their camper to sleep in overnight. Upon arrival, we were met with mounds of dirty dishes. Apparently, the water had been turned off for days. Hans explained that someone on behalf of the Nation was supposed to clear a blockage in the waste pipes but no one had come to do the job. There was no water to the house, and that meant no sewage. Find a tree!

The next morning, the sun was shining and the Churchill River was beckoning. Hans took a kayak and the rest of us grabbed canoes and lifejackets. I had a one-person canoe that I was not overly comfortable with, but the weather was calm and blissful. Marvin's daughter and boyfriend had never canoed before, and Marvin and his wife had canoed only a few times decades prior. Hans led the way and became affixed on Peterson Island, a gigantic rock he had named after himself. There was only room for his kayak to be pulled ashore, which he did and repeatedly dove off the rock into the frigid water. The rest of us decided to continue paddling across to the Stanley Mission Church and enjoyed an hour or two visiting the historic site.

I noticed clouds drawing in. We all headed back to our house on the peninsula. As we manoeuvred across the wide expanse of open water, the wind increased and the storm clouds turned to an ominous shade of grey. The clouds rumbled and finally the thunder and lightning broke free. The inexperienced canoeists were floundering; their faces told their fear. I was not much better. Hans was still playing on his rock, far in the distance, oblivious to our plight. Thankfully, we all wore life jackets.

"Paddle into the wind," I shouted at them across the whip of the wind. "Don't let your canoe be sideways to the wind! Zigzag! Zigzag, for Christ's sake, zigzag!"

By the time we all made it to shore, we were soaked to the bone and exhausted, but we were alive.

Marvin and his wife were first to pull ashore, and as I did the same, they raced back down to greet me, shouting, "We've been robbed!" Someone had broken into their camper and stolen all their food. More importantly, Marvin's prescription medications were nowhere to be seen.

As we all made our way back to our house, we noticed that our neighbour, Harry, and some friends were barbequing in his backyard. Harry's home was a collection of scrap lumber and tarps around a homemade wood stove. Most dog kennels were better built. I had taken Harry with me on my way back to the farm on different occasions, dropping him in La Ronge with his bags of recyclable cans he had collected. Harry had lots of issues. Hans had befriended him, which is probably the best thing he could have done. It wouldn't have been wise to make yourself Harry's enemy.

As we approached his backyard, we saw all our food and liquor splayed out on his table, which was a collection of one-metre-diameter circles of rough lumber with a centre core that had at one time been the spool to carry a roll of cable. Harry was drunk, and he went on a rant that he had killed his girlfriend, her body was down by the co-op store, he didn't mean to kill her, she pissed him off, he just wanted to show her who was boss. Now the RCMP was looking for him. He had taken the pills in Marvin's camper. What good were they? They didn't do anything for him! He was enjoying his last supper before they took him away. With a little luck he could eat and take off into the bush and they wouldn't find him.

I was horrified. We raced to the co-op store to look for his girlfriend. There were no RCMP anywhere. The clinic had a security guard, who escorted the nurses when they had to treat patients known to be difficult, and he told us that she had been taken away by medical staff before we got there.

We returned to our house to discover Hans, back from his swimming, and Harry and his friends were nowhere to be seen. I don't remember what we ate for dinner, maybe we didn't eat anything, that night, but we called it quits early. We left our door unlocked so that Marvin and his family could come inside if they needed to.

I woke up in the middle of the night because I heard someone moving in our house. Thinking it was Marvin, I got up and called out to him. It wasn't Marvin. Marvin is a huge, calm, cuddly teddy bear. It was totally dark but I could make out a person. The man in our house was wiry, erratic, irrational, jumping around like he had springs in his shoes.

"Hans owes me money," the man claimed. "I did work for him, he never paid me, I need my money!" He only had silky swim shorts on, and his chest showed each protruding rib. He was so hyper. I'm not sure how I collected myself, as Hans was sound asleep.

"I don't know where my glasses are," I said to him. "I can't pay you when I can't see anything. Come back in the morning, and I will pay you then." Somehow, the intruder bought my excuse.

At first light, as soon as Marvin and his family surfaced, I had my things in my car and left for home. Hans couldn't understand why I was leaving.

A couple of weeks later, I was speaking with my friend Jenn, who was a nurse at Stanley Mission Health Centre, and she explained that the young guy who was in our house that night had numerous criminal charges for assault and robbery. When he came into the clinic, they only treated him when the security officer was present. I never returned to Stanley Mission again, and I can only hope that Harry's girlfriend survived and moved on to a non-abusive relationship.

I have lived in poverty, but nothing like the impoverished situation I have witnessed in First Nations communities. I grew up in a council housing estate and became acutely aware of the haves and the have-nots within my own family and community, but I have come to understand that I avoided a certain level of poverty because I am white. I grew up with extremely racist parents in the UK. It was the era of "Rule Britannia." In school, when we learned about Canada, we saw visuals of wheat fields gently bending in a summer breeze. We also saw many visuals of Indigenous people, often in full traditional dress, their stoic, proud demeanour obvious for us all to see. It was years later that I would learn that this is a harmful stereotype.

When I immigrated to Canada, I had to attend interviews at Canada House in London, England, and the Canadian department of immigration showed me videos of the RCMP in full red dress standing on street corners and of Indigenous people wearing full regalia. It was decades after I arrived here that I realized how the Canadian government had misrepresented and used Indigenous Peoples. They didn't show me videos of how the RCMP rounded up and kidnapped Indigenous children to take them to residential schools or prohibited them from learning their own culture. The Canadian government wanted the country to appear to be a wonderful, harmonious place to foreigners.

I have witnessed what life is like in First Nations communities, and I still make mistakes. I used to think I could make a significant difference. It wasn't simply that I recognized I could not improve the quality of life in First Nations communities for the better. I also recognized that I was losing my impossible desire to change Hans. I couldn't dispute his passion to provide safe drinking water and, believe me, I felt that passion too. But I also recognized that this lifestyle was unhealthy for me, and I only managed to cope by living my solitary life at the farm. The magnitude of the problems I witnessed at Stanley Mission showed me a mountain of social injustice and the severity of the legacy of colonialism. It was much bigger than I could affect. Hans and I had tried for fifteen years, and we made a difference for so many. I was content with that and needed to regain control of my life.

19

West Coast Winters

In 2009, Hans succeeded in developing a biological wastewater treatment system for Stanley Mission. His new system was odourless and effective, and required minimal (if any) chemicals. He had met his goal of making safe drinking water a reality for many First Nations, and now wastewater treatment was a reality too.

It became operational shortly before he suffered a mental breakdown in December 2009. This moment was a rude awakening for me. Vascular dementia, caused by diabetes, had taken over his mind. I realized that the early effects of vascular dementia meant that he had not been difficult to work with when we hired a scientist for him to mentor because of his stubbornness or inflexibility; he had not been mentally capable of the communication required to pass on his knowledge. A beautiful bouquet arrived from Kawacatoose First Nations within a few hours of Hans's admittance to hospital. Other Indigenous communities kept him in their prayers and visited when they could.

Doctors ordered numerous blood samples to search for the cause of Hans's illness, and they called me in when they received the results. Hans seemed to have arsenic poisoning. Doctors quickly assumed he had been poisoned by the work he had undertaken in China and from sampling raw waters high in arsenic. That was simply not the case. Although he might have been untidy, Hans had impeccable laboratory procedures. I explained to doctors how Hans had been diagnosed with diabetes fifteen years earlier and had refused all conventional diabetic medications. I also explained how, when Hans came home from China, he returned with Chinese medicinal teas, which he steeped for hours before drinking many cups each day. Doctors sent the teas for analysis and, sure enough, the results demonstrated unbelievably high arsenic levels. The teas originated in the same region of China where Hans was advising the Chinese government on how to effectively remove arsenic from the raw water supply. If a tea plant on the other side of the world takes up the arsenic, why wouldn't cattle in Saskatchewan take up arsenic too?

When we first founded WRC, it was impossible to get liability insurance coverage for any company designing or building water treatment plants. The risk was too great. The best insurance we could get was "errors and omissions" coverage. When Hans was hospitalized, doctors declared he could no longer work, and his mental state meant we could not afford the risk of him making an error and having no insurance to cover us. This meant he was no longer covered for errors and omissions.

Sapphire Water International took over Hans's water treatment system and renamed it the Sapphire Integrated Biological and Reverse Osmosis Membrane, or SIBROM, treatment system.

Hans fell into a deep depression. He permanently moved to Stanley Mission after he was hospitalized. The slower pace, forests, nature and warmth of the people in the community were instrumental to his well-being and recovery.

⚔

Now that Hans was living at Stanley Mission, I had to decide what I was going to do. Sven and Elsa repeatedly told me, "Mum, you cannot keep living like this." I had devoted my life to supporting Hans and the SDWF from 1996 to 2009. We had no friends outside of work, no social life. We worked together while living apart. Selling the farm and moving away was my goal, but that was no easy task. Hans had become a hoarder; the barn and machine shed were full of unopened boxes of equipment he had purchased on eBay. Most of the packages contained non-functioning laboratory equipment, many items with tags stating what part needed to be ordered or re-placed. But before I could begin to conceive of how to deal with the farm, I needed to do something for myself.

In the summer of 2010, Elsa attended a week-long confer-ence in Shawnigan Lake on Vancouver Island and had invited me to bunk with her. I decided to finally begin taking care of myself and head west. We toured the island on the weekends. She told me she had a dream in which I lived on the island and had a huge garden full of flowers, and I was very happy. I had to agree that it sounded nice. My niece and goddaughter, who lived in Vancouver, found a rental suite for me: a tiny studio in Qualicum Beach that would wel-come me and my Old English Sheepdogs. That winter, I packed up my meagre belongings and made my way to my new home for the next four months.

Once again, my dear neighbours Wanda and Donny came to my rescue and blew out the water lines to the house to winterize them. On December 30, 2010, what would have been mine and Hans's twenty-seventh anniversary, I loaded up my 2004 Ford Freestar van. I took my computer, printer and important papers so I could continue working closely with Roger at Sapphire. I left a flat open space for my two Old English Sheepdogs, Bragi and Knut. Knut had never been away from the farm before and he had never even been on a leash. I had him neutered in time for the trip, hoping to make him a little easier to control, and I had found someone in Saskatoon who would take care of Sif, my oldest dog, for the winter. I had also taken my van in for a mechanical check prior to packing and everything was deemed A-one for the journey. I locked the door to the house and drove away. Adam changed the voice on my GPS to that of a man, jokingly claiming that if I wanted sound directions, I shouldn't trust a woman. Mark chatted with me as I made my way west.

December 30, 2010, was a typical, cold winter day, but there was bright sunshine and clear skies. I made good time to Edmon-ton, and I decided to keep driving to Hinton. I underestimated how far it was. The sunny skies began to fade, dusk descended and snow began to fall. The roads became slick, and oncoming headlights were mesmerizing. I told Mark that I was almost there, no need to chat again and I would let him know when I arrived in Hinton.

It happened fast, a flash in front of my driver window. It took me a few seconds, although it seemed much longer, before I realized what had occurred. My driver side windshield wiper had flown off into the cold white yonder. I slowed down as slushy ice formed in front of my eyes, obstructing my view of the road. I put on my hazard lights and crawled along on the side of the highway at a snail's pace. I kept my driver window down and reached out with a scraper trying to keep a small section clear of snow while also switching to look out of the passenger side windshield, where the wiper was still functioning. Every ten minutes I had to stop completely to clean the windshield.

At one of these stops I was taken by surprise: an old farm truck pulled up close behind me, and two old men, hefty characters wearing old ball caps, one with a red beard, offered to help me.

"Unless you have a spare wiper for a Freestar, I don't think you can do anything, thanks."

One of them suggested we go to the Legion, pointing to the distant lights, saying, "Jack for sure will have a wiper, and if not, then Joe will. Follow us back there and we'll get you fixed up and on your way."

I decided it was worth a try. It would take me all night to get to Hinton at this speed. I followed them to the Legion, poking my head inside after they entered. A group of very old men were playing cards and drinking. Through the haze of cigarette smoke I could see their wrinkled old eyes glistening at the thought of helping a damsel in distress. No one had a wiper blade that fit.

As I made my way back to the van, one of the men stood in my way, suggesting, "Come back to my place, you can sleep on my couch."

I took my cues from my dogs. Bragi was standing up front, her two front paws on the dashboard, barking aggressively. I don't think she had ever barked before. I knew she sensed danger. Knut was imitating his mum, not really knowing why, but he was upset too. A second man began walking toward me, and I moved quickly to get into my vehicle. As I opened my door, it was as much as I could do to hold Bragi in the vehicle.

One old man shouted at me, "Call your bloody dogs off."

"No way," I shouted back. "They are doing exactly what they are supposed to do." I locked all the doors and drove away, limping down the highway for a considerable distance, hardly able to see, yet too afraid to stop again.

Eventually, I made it to a 24-hour gas station, somewhere in the middle of nowhere, it seemed. The young cashier called his dad who came with a wiper and fixed my van. It was a five-minute job for the person with the right tools. I drove on my way, so very thankful for their help. And so very thankful for my dogs. I would make that trip for the next three winters, there and back. I hated the lonely drive and was always happy to have my dogs beside me.

From Hinton, I white-knuckled the whole way to Hope. The next night, New Year's Eve, Bragi, Knut and I celebrated the beginning of a new chapter in my life with new rawhide bones for them and pizza delivery to the Travelodge Hotel for me.

I made it to Qualicum Beach the next day, on the last ferry to cross that day due to rough seas. It felt good to reach my new home, a tiny garage converted into a studio suite of less than four hundred square feet.

I had mixed emotions every single day. Often every hour. Trying to build a new life in a completely strange community, completely alone, when you are sixty years old is no easy task. I cried a great deal. Thankful every day for my dogs, I took them for long walks morning and night. Knut had run free on the farm for his first three years. He had as difficult a time adjusting to our new surroundings as I did.

I volunteered at a charity café and registered for art classes. It was as much as I could do to push myself to attend but I enjoyed meeting new people. I went to the local pool and joined aquacise classes, where a group of ladies took me under their wings, inviting me for coffee after each session. I was desperate to make friends. I was a wreck. Women recognized my raw emotional state and offered their support. We shared jokes, bitched and laughed often, the very best medicine. The exercises at the pool, accompanied by some great oldies music, lifted me physically and emotionally. I also contacted a nearby care home and offered to bring Bragi, as she was a registered therapy dog. We visited the clients two or three times a week. While I enjoyed my time and was so proud of Bragi, I found this the hardest activity. So many clients with dementia reminded me of Hans or his mother, Asta. Eventually, I had to stop the visits.

It felt so wonderful to have so many female friends again. Elsa often came to visit me, and I relished our time together. At the end of April, I planned to head back to Saskatchewan, but delayed it almost a month longer to enjoy a visit with Elsa and hopefully have better road conditions. My children remained the focal point of my life. My new life in BC was beginning—but first I had three summers ahead of me of tirelessly cleaning up the farm to sell it.

When I returned to the farm in the summers, I toiled from sun-up until sundown, day after day after day. Once again, my angel of a neighbour came to my rescue and her sons helped me with the physical work. It took me from April until October each summer, working methodically through the mess. Hoses of various lengths and diameters had been stored along fence lines of the many corrals; they were heavy and cumbersome, and pulling them out from under more than one season's growth of weeds and grass was not easy. Then there were boxes and plastic tubs loaded to overflowing with valves. They all had to be sorted and catalogued to prepare for sale. There were also the boxes of disposable razors from when Hans was upset at the price of razors and calculated that he could buy a lifetime supply for a pittance. Boxes of gloves and mitts, parkas and VHS tapes from a video store. I had always believed him when he purchased the lab equipment. I had been so overwhelmed running the SDWF and the farm and raising my beautiful children that I had never stopped to look inside his purchases. Now I had to find homes for everything. Value Village in Saskatoon took truckloads. I contacted medical charities working in developing countries and that led to a retired scientist volunteering to help me. He went through the lab equipment, obtained manuals, decided if it could be rebuilt or was garbage and, whenever possible, repaired the item. Each item that had some life left in it went to the various interested charities in return for tax receipts. We filled three forty-foot containers and one twenty-foot container with garbage.

Hans had an extensive collection of peer-reviewed academic papers and journals and a library of over five thousand books relating to water treatment processes. I spent hours listing all the books by title and author. The University of Saskatchewan was keen to take over the collection. I packed everything in boxes labelled alphabetically, then the boxes went into a trailer we had once used for moving large pieces of equipment to and from the various First Nations communities. At the last minute before I took them to Saskatoon, Hans was adamant, he needed the library with him at Stanley Mission, and so that is where it went. I often wonder what happened to that valuable collection.

Disposing of the chemicals was a huge ordeal, as I had to get transportation approval and then pay huge fees to drop them at a specific location in Saskatoon. Driving with them loaded in my vehicle was a very worrying trip. The final bill for disposal was thousands of dollars.

During these years, I relied heavily on Sven's ex-girlfriend Jenn and her mother, Gail. Two more angels in my life. I could not have got through this period without their wonderful support. Gail was a social worker and often acted as my sounding board, guiding my ability to remain strong, encouraging me to look after myself first. It was coincidence that Jenn also worked occasionally as a nurse at Stanley Mission and could also offer support to Hans. She checked on him as often as she was able to. She played her dual role with sensitivity, genuine concern and with the expertise of her training. I can never thank them enough for all they did for me.

As his memory slowly started to improve, we soon discovered that Hans was not ready to quit living and breathing water treatment. His scientific ability for calculations, as well as his insight, candor, wit and ability to document the issues never wavered up to the day he died, despite his memory failing in other ways. He was able to start over, to some degree, still working with First Nations, still giving presentations, still making a positive difference, all while I was cleaning up the farm. I had often likened working with Hans to working in the eye of a tornado, but now I felt like I was cleaning up after the tornado had passed through. These were tumultuous years. I desperately wanted a divorce. It was complicated and weighed heavy on our children.

One day, Hans called me. "Sue, I need your help. I've bought a new car, and I get to drive it away, but I don't know what to do with my old Durango. Can you come and drive it back to Saskatoon for me?" He wasn't supposed to be spending or working. It was impossible to stop him from doing either.

"I am living on Vancouver Island now. No, I can't come help you. You had no business buying a new car, you must figure it out. You should have thought this through." We hung up, and it seemed within seconds that he called me back.

"No problem, I know what I can do. I will give the Durango to my girlfriend. She doesn't have a car, so I'll give it to her."

Hans's solution cut me to my core. When we first met, I was driving an old, unreliable Toyota Corolla hatchback. Hans had convinced me I should buy a newer, more reliable vehicle, and we found a Mazda 326. I went to the bank to work out financing, and when I returned to the dealership to sign final papers, I was shocked: Hans had already paid for my car. I felt so special and appreciated when he made this gift to me, but hearing his plan thirty years later, I felt replaced. I was exhausted from all the legal ramifications. I had no more energy left, neither emotional nor physical. Amazingly, soon after this, Hans began cooperating with our divorce, which was finalized October 30, 2014.

My first winter in BC, I met Carol at the swimming pool, and we had become close friends. The first year I returned to Saskatchewan, I received the sad news that Judy, one of Carol's friends, had passed away suddenly from a brain aneurism. When I returned the following winter, I spent time with Carol and her friends as before, but they also included Judy's partner, Roelof. We both had seemingly insurmountable grief, we understood each other's triggers, the anniversaries, birthdays—the little things that meant so much.

Early in 2016, I was in a shopping mall when my cell phone rang. I was surprised that Sven was calling me on a Friday midday, so I picked up quickly. Ever since Sven had left for Europe, he had returned for many spontaneous visits, but he also called regularly, and always at the right moment, as if he knew when I needed to hear his voice. Perhaps it was an insight or sixth sense. This Friday, though, his call was out of the blue.

"What's up?" I asked.

"Just checking to see if you got an invite to the family wedding," he said, laughing hard.

"Whatever are you talking about?"

"I just got off the phone with Dad, and he can't understand why I can't be in Saskatoon tomorrow to be at his wedding. Apparently, he is marrying a lady from Jamaica. It must be a rush; I think he is saving her from being deported."

We laughed together. Life had become so complicated, and we had learned that we had to laugh at Hans's antics.

"Nope, I didn't get an invite, but do ask Elsa if she did. Oh well, I didn't have a suitable dress to wear anyway." We chuckled some more and said our goodbyes.

20

Hans's Passing

In October of 2018, Elsa called me, sobbing: Hans had been rushed to the hospital in an ambulance and the paramedics were not sure if they could save him. He had suffered a heart attack, another complication of untreated diabetes. Adam had found him and called the ambulance. I shared their grief, their memories. An hour later, she called me back with the devastating news. How I wished I could have convinced him to take diabetic medications.

For the next five days, I searched boxes to find VHS tapes of his various media interviews, I scanned numerous family photo albums and set up Kodak slides on a light desk to select those to show at his funeral. Luckily, I found a man an hour away who offered to transpose all the 8 mm and VHS tapes and slides into digital files. I busily scanned the photos myself and couriered a portable drive loaded with Hans's life, our life, to our son in Saskatoon. I watched the funeral remotely from my home on the island. In his heartfelt eulogy for his father, Sven told the story of how Hans took him and Elsa canoeing when they were young. Hans had only packed a tin of beef stew and a packet of Norwegian goat cheese and crispbread, and neither he nor Elsa have been able to eat either since. Everyone chuckled. That was so typical for Hans. Sven described his father then as "the most unreasonable, most unique person I have ever met." I couldn't have agreed more.

I recalled my extreme anxiety and frustrations listening to the countless Indigenous communities begging for us to help them, their stories of neglect by all levels and colours of government and the nonchalant indifference toward helping Indigenous communities by too many potential funders. I was motivated to help as best I could with as much energy and passion as Hans.

Engineers have told me that Hans had spent the year before he passed drafting new water quality regulations for First Nations in Saskatchewan. The project was headed by a lady named Rebecca and overseen by a committee of First Nations people and scientists. Hans hoped these new standards would compel INAC to install better treatment plants on First Nations reserves. I have been unable to locate anyone who worked with him on this venture, although Hans is quoted in *The Globe and Mail* as saying the Indigenous Affairs department, to which he presented these guidelines, is "pissed off."[99]

Hans directly impacted over twenty First Nations communities, which I believe would still be on boil water advisories if not for his dedication. When on site, Hans worked eighteen-hour days, seven days a week. He lived at the Yellow Quill First Nation from July 2002 to April 2004, the Saddle Lake Cree Nation from 2004 to 2007, and at Stanley Mission from 2007 to 2009. When he continued living in the Stanley Mission area, the community benefitted from many other changes that Hans encouraged, such as kayaking, snowshoeing and cross-country skiing social clubs. Hans also improved the choice of healthy foods available at the local store as part of his efforts to educate about diabetes.

The operators that Hans had trained in various communities gained confidence and understanding, and immediately wanted to support other communities that struggled with the consequences of ineffective water treatment systems. Thus, the Advanced

Aboriginal Water Treatment Team (AAWTT) which was created in 2006 and continues Hans's legacy through their advocacy. Bob Pratt, the water treatment operator at George Gordon First Nation in Saskatchewan, was the driving force and ongoing inspiration for this group. His community's water was too high in everything, including arsenic, organics, iron, manganese, sulphate and hardness. He tried the straight manganese greensand filtration and reverse osmosis system, but it simply didn't work. In 2005, the community received an IBROM processing plant, and his community now has water that meets all global regulations. Operational costs for the plant dropped by $100,000 per year.[100] The AAWTT operators passed their official operator licensing requirements and wanted to share their knowledge and advice with other communities' water treatment operators. Sharing their knowledge with fellow water treatment operators became paramount.

One AAWTT operator, Deon Hassler, recipient of the 2019 National First Nations Water Leadership Award, had this to say about his experience being mentored by Hans:

> Dr. Hans, I first met him around 2004 when he was building/developing the IBROM system at Pasqua First Nation. Dr. Hans mentored me in the IBROM system. He communicated with me every day in the last year or two of his life. He was discussing and sharing his work with me on the IBROM system. Around 2017, I attended a Water Security Agency meeting with him to present the IBROM system. He later sent me to the village of Lemberg which had ammonia issues in their drinking water. I presented the SIBROM system to the mayor and council and discussed options of a pilot project. To this present day, I use this experience in my daily job as a Circuit Rider Trainer for File Hills Qu'Appelle Tribal Council to mentor, train water plant operators, and educate leadership on the IBROM system in eleven First Nations communities. ...

I am grateful for the time I spent with Dr. Hans. It was an honour learning from his expertise. To this day, I continue to carry on his teachings to the best of my ability. I will forever be thankful for the mentorship I received from Dr. Hans and to the SDWF team for bringing me on.[101]

Roberta Neapetung, the water treatment operator in Yellow Quill, also wrote a statement for Hans:

I've worked with Dr. Hans Peterson as a Water Keeper. Dr. Hans's passion for water flowed into me with every story and lesson he shared with us water keepers. Dr. Hans was a very smart, funny and kind man to learn from. He gave me confidence in my job to say and know what I am doing as a biological water plant operator. His passion for water became a part of me, and my understanding of his work.

He taught me my love for my job. He was a great man for me to know and I want to convey that in my statement. It was a pleasure to work with Dr. Hans and his crew. I was an operator for Yellow Quill First Nation for thirteen years. I've been an operator for the Key First Nation for five years, so eighteen years all together. The Key First Nation is getting a new bio plant based on my skills to run it properly and I'm excited to get started again. Thank you.[102]

Hans would be especially humbled and honoured to learn of the Hans Peterson Operator Award given out annually by the Saskatchewan First Nations Water Association (SFNWA). He was impressed, time and time again, with each First Nations community he worked with. Some individuals were passionate, committed and prepared to go the extra mile for the greater good of their community. Hans described these people as being *keen*. He loved *keen* people. Now, in his honour, the winner of this award is chosen from the list of worthy nominees annually by the board members of the SFNWA. Anyone can nominate an individual they believe is worthy of the award. Every person whose name is put forward is a credit to Hans's legacy.

21

Hans's Legacy: Bucking the System

In 2006, Hans wrote an article for the *Aboriginal Times*, beginning it with this statement:

> Earlier this year, CBC radio broadcast a national documentary called *Slow Boil* that investigated water quality issues in Aboriginal communities. That same morning, I fielded ten live interviews from different regions through the CBC broadcast centre in Saskatoon. Later that day, the INAC Minister Jim Prentice pledged he would deal with unsafe drinking water on First Nation communities across the country. That hasn't happened yet, but a federal inquiry has been touring the country getting feedback from Indigenous communities on water issues. Some of the questions: "Should we have drinking water guidelines or regulations? Should those regulations/guidelines be enforced by the province in which the community is located or by the federal government?" This is just smoke and mirrors.[103]

Seventeen years later, I still see smoke and mirrors from our federal government. In 2005, he wrote, "Will existing rural surface water treatment systems meet guidelines in ten to twenty years from now? Not likely!"[104] He was right again! Still today, I believe that science is the missing link. We desperately need to have independent, unbiased scientists who can assess, detail and prove scientifically why some water treatment systems are ineffective and others are not. We need national drinking water regulations more than ever. There are no better regulations to adhere to than those set by the WHO. We don't need to reinvent the regulations; we just need to adhere to them.[105]

I remained involved with the SDWF and worked with Roger Chapman of Sapphire International until 2013 to ensure that all communities awaiting IBROM systems received them. This was only made possible by Roger's constant dedication, and the hard work of many employees of Sapphire International. Eventually, Sapphire sold the SIBROM system to Delco Water, which has since adapted the design. It is now a two-vessel system (instead of three), with "anthracite in place of Filtralite, too much unnecessary instrumentation, pH media/chemicals, high air/oxygen, frequent RO cleaning, RO concentration plugging sewer lines and there may be a few more."[106] Filtralite is the media of choice for IBROMs to work effectively, the media which outperformed all others during the years of on-site testing that Hans measured. Anthracite is a cheaper replacement for Filtralite, but it falls short of equal performance or effectiveness. A water treatment operator says that he has "seen the changes the engineering companies and Delco Water have made to the IBROM system and is annoyed with those changes." Because Hans did not leave a scientific will, many feel there is no legacy to build upon. As Roger said to me soon after Hans passed away, "His knowledge died with him. Like the rest of us, I am sure Hans thought he would be around for a long time." Even before Delco purchased the system, Sapphire charged too much for municipalities to be able to afford it. Now, the Delco design is also too expensive: as an anonymous source told me, "Hans constantly went from plant to plant solving problems and keeping the systems operating free of charge. That is no longer the case. Delco charges for everything, and they charge a lot." Hans's confrontation of these issues helped influence progress, and without that push, "things have drifted backward." At the same time, "Hans pissed off a lot of people by being confrontational and aggressive. It was necessary but has had lasting effects."

I invited Delco to preview my memoir and contribute stories and information, but they informed me that their purchase of the system was an "asset purchase," that any historical record is the property of Mancal and that they cannot provide any information. Two critical words: *asset purchase*. Of course, when corporations invest in buying assets, they do it with the primary goal of profit.

There are some positive developments: Deon Hassler, a water treatment operator and member of AAWTT says that in 2019, the AAWTT "convinced Indigenous Services Canada (ISC) to build biological water treatment plants by lowering the cost. We now have approximately thirty biological water treatment plants in First Nation communities and at least three in non-First Nation communities, with more on the way this year."[107] Biological treatment plants are still being developed, and this is, perhaps, in large part due to the awareness that Hans and the SDWF brought to the issue.

The SFNWA was a concept and a vision that Hans initiated between 2017 and 2018 prior to his passing, and according to its website, its mission is to "strengthen capacity at the community level for the care and management of water on First Nations land."[108] In June of 2023, I received the SFNWA newsletter, which spoke about the three latest people to be hired by the organization: an engagement coordinator, a program coordinator and an administrative assistant. I have challenges determining how people in these positions affect the quality of water in First Nations. What they need is a scientist. In my network of those involved with water issues and government, the frustrations among us can be summed up by this comment:

> I doubt that SFNWA would hire anyone that is going to buck the system. So again, we see more funds thrown at First Nations drinking water, which does nothing to change the situation and actually provide safe drinking water to their communities.[109]

I also noted in the newsletter that three of the IBROM communities, Gordon, Whitecap and Yellow Quill, now have BWAs in effect. An uninformed person may assume that the water treatment operators are slacking in their responsibilities. But I know these operators, I know that isn't the case. I asked around for what had happened after, in the case of Yellow Quill, twenty years of unfaltering operation. Here is the response I received:

> I just talked to a guy that has been at these plants and the problems are leaks in the distribution system, lack of maintenance and expansion where required, and INAC failed to fix the issues.

This doesn't surprise me in the least. A common recurring problem is that INAC may fund specific projects, but they do not fund adequate maintenance of those projects. It is then easy and fitting within colonial ideology to blame the Indigenous people for not maintaining the projects. My anonymous source continued:

> Perhaps the engineering companies do have their value systems... but are apprehensive to build IBROMs as they are concerned operators may not fully accept their responsibilities. They did great with Hans at the helm, but he did more than build effective water treatment systems. He changed the way science was taught and how self-esteem and confidence building was part of the system.

Although I am not aware of any audited financial statements for the organization prior to 2021, the SFNWA financial statements from 2022 can be found on their website. In their audited statements for the year ending March 31, 2022, they show no cost of wages or salaries and show less than $10,000 in revenue for 2021, $4,500 of which comes from memberships. However, for 2022, their revenue leaps to over $500,000, with zero from memberships and $550,000 coming from Indigenous Services Canada (ISC), what used to be the INAC. Deferred revenue of a similar amount leads me to think that they received the same amount from the ISC in 2023; funding from the ISC thus totals over one million dollars over the past two years. I was surprised to see this disclaimer: "the Association receives majority of its revenue pursuant to funding agreements with Indigenous Services Canada. Should any of the funding be discontinued, it would greatly affect the operations." I have never seen such a statement on any audited financial statements for a charity or non-profit before.

While I believe the SFNWA is the result of Hans's dream and passion, their current operating procedures are far from anything he would have endorsed. Perhaps many things have changed in the decade since I retired, but when I was running the SDWF, CRA required a specific percentage of revenue to be spent on services in accordance with the mission of the organization to maintain charitable status. I believe the SFNWA operates as a non-profit and has applied for charitable status. I can't help but recall how CRA, in my opinion, harassed us for four years with audit after audit.

I have learned about a lavish Christmas party the SFNWA put on for their board members and staff which apparently lasted a full day. While those in attendance did participate in a board meeting that afternoon, it also included lunch, hors d'oeuvres at a hotel in the late afternoon, a ride in a stretch limo through the Enchanted Forest, a Christmas light display in Saskatoon, and touring private homes light displays before stopping at Saskatoon's most expensive steakhouses for dinner. They then toured the new offices they are currently remodelling—incurring renovation costs, my source suspects, that may be close to $169,000. A brief reminder here that there are still First Nations communities with decades-old boil water advisories, others that should be on BWAs and aren't, that there are mothers who cannot bathe their children in their tap water for fear they might swallow some, that individuals are continuing to suffer from rare forms of cancer, asthma, skin rashes—the list goes on. I find it unacceptable that those gifted with the funds to make safe drinking water a reality in First Nations chose to spend money in this way. I wonder what stipulations INAC applied to their funding?

Maybe another donor has stepped forward to cover the cost of their staff parties.

The SFNWA Annual General Meeting in 2023 offered wonderful cultural experiences like teepee raising. We cannot move forward without traditional Indigenous knowledge, but we also need sound unbiased scientific knowledge. Maybe I am wrong to expect that from an organization like the SFNWA. If INAC gave this money to SFNWA to encourage the much-needed Indigenous knowledge, to incorporate the cultural, spiritual and relational significance of water in First Nations communities, then INAC's mission was fulfilled. I would like to know if INAC gave equal—or any—funding to SFNWA to use science toward providing safe drinking water to Indigenous communities.

On December 11, 2023, Indigenous Services Minister Patty Hajdu introduced Bill C-61, intended to "to protect fresh water sources, create minimum national drinking water and wastewater *standards* in First Nations and provide sustainable funding for maintaining water quality."[110] The federal government claims it consulted with the Assembly of First Nations and held other consultations over the years to help inform the bill, but it will not release a list of the Nations consulted. The CBC reports that Chief Chris Moonias of Neskantaga First Nation was not consulted, and his community, four hundred and fifty kilometres north of Thunder Bay and only accessible by plane, has had the longest boil water advisory in Canada: twenty-eight years.[111] Time will tell how the new "sustainable funding" provided by the bill will be distributed.

In my opinion, effective water treatment systems will become a reality when First Nations are empowered to assume full responsibility for their community drinking water, which means assuming control of all contracts for water and wastewater treatment plants in their own communities. However, there must also be national drinking water *regulations,* not standards or guidelines, applicable to all Canadians. Regulations are enforceable by law, requiring a regulator to oversee and take legal action when required. This will also address incompetent, or deceitful, water treatment operators, like those in Walkerton and of which there are undoubtedly more.

For decades, I had expected a class action lawsuit against the federal government and INAC. As I mentioned in my introduction, I was happy to discover that it is now possible for First Nations to make claim for the approved settlement between Canada and certain First Nations.[112] Yet to repeat myself, I see potential significant issues with the language of the settlement. First, what if Indigenous communities require more than the allocated funds? While the settlement does say "*at least* $6 billion to support construction, upgrading, operation and maintenance of water and wastewater infrastructure in First Nations communities,"[113] we all know how major projects can multiply in cost from initial projections. A better agreement would be that the federal government agrees to pay for *all* necessary systems to be upgraded to meet or exceed the most stringent of either *all* Canadian drinking water guidelines or WHO's water quality guidelines.

My second concern relates to the fact that registering for this claim negates any future claims. What if First Nations folks register and accept a trivial or insulting amount for a settlement, and then the more significant part of the offering is delayed? Elder Raymond Tony Charlie describes how this happened to him in his memoir *In the Shadow of the Red Brick Building*: he received a fraction of what he was expecting in the settlement, yet he had signed an agreement that said he could no longer pursue his case. He had no other options.[114] Let's not forget what is behind this federal offering. I believe it is simply the cheapest option, as they have done for decades, be it with water treatment or housing, the cheapest way out is all they adhere to. It is my earnest hope that those who wish for sound legal advice before entering this contract can obtain it.

Although there has been some progress in recent years, including a legislative proposal for laws and regulations for safe drinking water in First Nations communities,[115] at the time of writing, there are twenty-eight long-term BWA on reserves, some of which have been in place for more than twenty-five years. As the Council of Canadians' website states, the "lack of clean, safe drinking water in

First Nations is one of the greatest violations of the UN-recognized human rights to water and sanitation."[116] The time to act is now; it was the time to act in 1996.

I think back to 1983, when Mark affectionately wrote on his classroom chalkboard "The Mad Scientist" in reference to Hans. Let's consider the different possible meanings of *mad*. If Hans could come back today, he would not be a *crazy* scientist. He would be livid, incensed, annoyed, irate, infuriated, exasperated, enraged—he would be a *furious* scientist indeed. *Mad* would be an understatement. Hans used his rage to effect change as best he could. This, too, is his legacy.

Conclusion

I am encouraged by the appearance of improvements for many Indigenous communities during the past decade under the Liberal government. I continue to feel we still have a long way to go, but at least we are on the right path.

To me, a "drinking water advisory" is being told to drink eight glasses of water a day. It is a very different message than a BWA. A "boil water advisory" is much more serious: you must boil every drop of water to bathe babies, brush teeth, cook and clean fridges. I feel it is a ploy to downplay the seriousness of the issue. I imagine that individuals may not heed the critical nature of a DWA, and that public health is at risk.

While the government talks about introducing drinking water standards and has proudly proclaimed that many First Nations communities now meet these government standards, they are only implementing their own government standards, far lower than those recommended by the WHO. Why not accept the WHO standards as the new bar? To quote Elizabeth May,

> While most Canadians have been scandalized by the lack of safe drinking water for Indigenous communities, few know that for settler culture Canadians as well, we have no regulations to ensure our drinking water is safe. We are the only industrialized nation without regulations to ensure safe drinking water. To this day, toxins and other contaminates in our water are subject only to guidelines and not legally enforceable standards.[117]

After all, this is a basic human right.

More importantly, unless drinking water standards become regulations, they really don't make much, if any, improvement over the existing guidelines. I have deep concern for the many rural communities who are under BWAs. They do not have the resources or unified clout of falling under the responsibility of the federal government.

I believe that too many of the old guards still remain in government departments like INAC and that they are embedded within too many consulting and engineering companies. I believe funds have been ineffectively allocated by INAC creating an illusion that monies have helped First Nations with improved effective water treatment systems, but this hasn't been reality.

My most critical concern lies with First Nations communities being given full responsibility for their own drinking water. While this is the right—and the only—way forward, I believe they are being set up for failure and I foresee that with an impending change of government the rhetoric will become *See? We knew you couldn't take responsibility.*

Because scientists haven't been involved, I have no faith that both community source waters and/or treated waters have been adequately tested. Therefore, many communities have systems that are incapable of producing safe drinking water—that is water which meets at minimum *all* parameters of the Canadian drinking water guidelines and therefore should still be under BWAs. First Nations are working with a broken corrupt system and ineffective infrastructure; unless they can replace both they are doomed to fail. But I am not a scientist; I just lived with the most passionate scientist there is on this topic.

If First Nations chiefs can unite and stand strong, and make these demands, then all Canadians will benefit, and it can become the true basis of reconciliation. To quote Yellow Quill First Nation Chief John Machiskinic:

> Dr. Hans Peterson was an ally to the nation. Our
> message to other First Nations Leaders is to search

for those allies, not just consultants, but experts that care because they will go the distance for your people. Our message to Canadians is to be those allies because if First Nations communities thrive, so does Canada.

It was a rare opportunity for us to share an afternoon paddling on the South
Saskatchewan River.

My therapy garden continues to be a place of joy and relaxation.

Epilogue

The Garden of Elsa's Dream

I now see my past as someone else's, someone I don't recognize any-more. I feel as though I am living Elsa's dream. The time that this memoir covers has left an indelible mark on my soul, and on my heart. Writing and sharing these years has helped tremendously.

I saw a sign displayed at the entrance to the Neskantaga First Nation community. In painted black letters, on rough-hewn wooden boards, it said simply, and accurately, "Broken promis-es, broken lives, broken families." We shared the pain of so many communities. I believe everyone in our family has been affected and we all continue to do the best we can, in our own ways, to heal and move on.

Roelof and I built our own version of Butchart Gardens. With local garden clubs and nurseries holding plant sales, we went crazy. But my most treasured plants are those received from friends. To-day, we have over three thousand bulbs and seven hundred peren-nial plants. We have given away or sold thousands of pots of plants each spring to neighbours and fellow gardeners. I like to think I am living up to my Nana's saying, "The front garden is to feed the souls of people passing by." So many people stop to tell us how much joy our garden gives them. Gardens are for sharing. With my hands in the soil—or holding a paint brush, a sketching pencil, or writing my story—I have been able to move on.[118]

Roelof has consistently kept me wined and dined. After all the years of doing so many jobs on the farm, often ones that I would have preferred not to do, now I live like a princess, rarely even taking out the garbage! I pinch myself each day that I can be this lucky, living here in paradise. I have hung two signs on our back fence that display words I like to live by. One is from Mark: "Some people try to turn back their odometers, but not me. I want people to know why I look this way. I've travelled a long way, and a lot of the roads weren't paved." The other is from Elsa: "Your mind is a garden. Your thoughts are the seeds. You can grow flowers, or you can grow weeds."

I have moved on in my own way, but I continue to try to make a difference. I read, I read all I can, and I have included a Recommended Reading list in the Appendix. I often contact my MP to share my opinion and insist on national drinking water regulations, or my MLA over impending issues that I believe are not being handled as they should be. I continue to support the SDWF and the Keepers of the Water. I try to become aware of which companies or individuals have invested in Big Oil and I boycott them. I have selected investment strategies that removed my investments out of the hands of banks or companies where CEOs take home exorbitant amounts of money through funding and otherwise supporting Big Oil. I am lobbying to have my bank and pension fund exclude financing or investing in Big Oil. I discuss these issues with my social network as often as I can. Roelof and I fly an Indigenous flag. It is not enough for me to acknowledge that I am on unceded territory. I feel I am saying, "I know we stole this from you, but so be it." I am searching for what I can add to this statement in solidarity with First Nations. So far, my way of acknowledging is to state: I give thanks to First Nations for both allowing and enabling me to live a life of privilege on their lands. I try to acknowledge my appreciation of this gift by standing in solidarity on the myriad of issues where they have been wronged. In part, writing this book is my declaration that I stand in solidarity with Indigenous Peoples in Canada. I do not profess to have all the answers. I hope that by sharing what I know with others, many will open their eyes and minds to new ways of thinking, processing what they learn or need to unlearn and pressure those in positions of power to step up and take appropriate action.

Please join me in demanding the following inquiries. First, an inquiry into the distribution of funds by the SFNWA, which I believe should lead to a national inquiry into the ISC, what was INAC, and how they have distributed taxpayer money with little or no accountability.

Second, an inquiry into all engineering contracts awarded with the intent to provide safe drinking water to Neskantaga First Nation, the community with Canada's longest standing BWA of twenty-eight years. I believe the outcome of this will demand a further national inquiry into all funds INAC has distributed to engineers with the same intent. Most of these contracts have not accomplished this goal.

Neither Hans nor I ever accepted any payment from the SDWF for any of our advocacy work. I intend to maintain this record by pledging to donate all royalties earned from sales of this book in Canada to the Safe Drinking Water Foundation and the Keepers of the Water.

Acknowledgements

I believe now more than ever that things happen for a reason and, if it is meant to be, it will be. While I lived this period of my life in isolation, I have been enabled and encouraged to share it by incredibly supportive people. I give my sincere and humble gratitude to so many.

The impetus of this book is the work of my late ex-husband, Hans, his research, innovation and devotion to developing effective water treatment systems and to educating all Canadians. I hope you can hear his voice, his sense of humour, his ability to write in scathingly honest terms and his unending support for Indigenous Peoples in Canada.

My deepest gratitude to our daughter, Elsa, for encouraging me to begin writing my life story twelve years ago. Without her inspiration, I would not have begun this journey.

Thanks to my friends, one of whom read my initial notes and said, "You have a story here, a good story, a book. Focus on these fifteen years." She gave me the encouragement and confidence to continue writing. Without her words of encouragement, I would still be thinking of myself as what my English teacher in secondary school ingrained in me when he made me repeat to the class one hundred times, "I am a ninny."

When on a garden tour one day, I unexpectedly met Liane Mahugh. She edited initial drafts and helped me set up my website. Her support has been instrumental in allowing my writing to become what it is today. Without her, this book would not have reached fruition.

Sincere thanks to Nicole Hancock, Executive Director of the Safe Drinking Water Foundation, for her dedication to this issue, her keen eye for detail, her record keeping and her support. Thanks also to the Keepers of the Water for their support and unrelenting pursuit of justice for Indigenous Peoples.

When I contacted people with whom I hadn't communicated for over a decade, I was overwhelmed at their generosity. Some sobbed into the phone, "Thank you for telling our story," or, "I cried into my coffee this morning, I am so happy you are writing this." I couldn't have shared my stories without their permission and encouragement.

To Roberta Neapetung, water treatment operator at Yellow Quill First Nation, and Deon Hassler, recipient of the 2019 National First Nations Water Leadership Award: thank you for trusting me with representing your stories. To all the Indigenous people, and to the many non-Indigenous folks, including engineers, civil servants, politicians and farmers who cannot be quoted, thank you from the bottom of my heart for trusting me with your anonymity. I look forward to the day when all of those living on the land we refer to as Canada can speak freely.

To Dr. John O'Connor and Dr. Mark Torchia, current and former board members of the Safe Drinking Water Foundation, respectively, thank you for believing in me. Your passion and support empowered me to keep writing.

When I wanted feedback from beta readers, I thought, who better to ask than my own book club friends? Now, when can you ever get ten women to agree on a single point of view? When you ask them all to be beta readers. Ten ladies laughed with me, cried with me and guided me toward becoming comfortable as they requested that I "show more about myself." With their encouragement, I have attempted to do just that.

I am forever thankful to Warren Goulding, author of *Just Another Indian*. When I reached out to him, he generously gave me his time and mentored me to seek a publisher. Without his belief in me and my story, this could not have materialized.

As a result of Warren's suggestions, I contacted Caitlin Press, and I was humbled when publisher Vici Johnstone replied to my email inquiry saying I had piqued her interest. Caitlin Press is committed to its feminist origins by publishing bold works by and about BC women, for a local and national readership. Thank you, Vici, for seeing me as fitting within your mission, for giving so much of yourself and your team to make my writing readable. As Vici introduced me to her publishing team Sarah Corsie and Malaika Aleba, all three ladies blew me away with their expertise and professionalism. That is when I accepted that this was no longer a dream; it really was happening to me.

When I began working on editing my manuscript with Caitlin's developmental editor Holly Vestad, I felt I had truly arrived in the most capable hands in the publishing industry. Holly's sensitivity, efficiency and genuine interest in my story, her guidance, her patience and her unique ability to make my story flow to engage the reader, never failed to amaze me. Holly played with my manuscript as though she was fine-tuning a precious instrument, and she played it so beautifully; I hope the world will want to listen. When it was Sarah's turn to lead a sensitivity/copy edit, I had no idea where her questions and suggestions were rooted. I quickly gained a great appreciation for how she had my back and brought even more clarity to my stories. Thank you, Sarah. As I begin my journey with Malaika, she too has applied her fabulous skills in marketing and promoting my book, boosting all my hopes and dreams. I am so grateful for the entire Caitlin team publishing my memoir in just eight months.

There is one more man to whom I give thanks every day: my partner, Roelof, who has never questioned my need to revisit and expose my past. He has kept me fully stocked with wine, fresh baked delicacies, breakfasts, lunches and dinners so that I could sit and write. At the same time, we have both gained so much joy from our love of gardening together.

When I moved to Vancouver Island, I was intent on one important focus in my new life. That was to never again let my female friends slip away, to always hold my women friends close to my heart. I feel blessed to have so many women supporting and encouraging me every step of the way.

Lastly, I wish to thank you, the reader, as there is no value in writing a book unless people take time to read it. Thank you, each one of you.

Appendix One

Ontario First Nations
Technical Services Memo

**ONTARIO FIRST NATIONS TECHNICAL
SERVICES CORPORATION**

RE: Mr. John Hookimaw' House in Attawapiskat

TO: Kevin Atkins, Brian Holmes and Art Mauro

CC: Mr. Derek Etherington, Jacqueline Hookimaw, Craig Nootchtal
Musghkeqowuk, Irving Leblanc, P.Eng, Gilles St. Pierre, Mike Gull,

FROM: Derrick Kamanga, M. Eng, and P.Eng: OFNTSC

DATE: Thursday, 09 June 2005

RE: Mr. John Hookimaw's House

Topic: Sewage backup flooding.

Background:

Prior to April, 15, Mr. John Hookimaw and his family experienced sewage
back-up into the crawl space of his house. Inspection and reports have
been undertaken by Mushkegowuk Council Technical Services, Health
Canada-Environmental Health Officer and Attawapiskat First Nations
Technical Services Unit.

We all agree that the house must be vacated and boarded-up. The cause
of the sewer back-up cannot be defiantly determined without a feasibility
report. However, what is currently known is that DeBeers discharged a
load of sewage into the pumping station. This might have precipitated the
overloading of the pumping station, thereby causing sewage back-up. In
addition the First Nation administration does not have a sewer- connection
plumbing standard or by-law. It is alleged that all this may have
contributed somewhat to this unfortunate episode.

In addition, the First Nation is planning a submission within the community
which will exert further demand on the existing sewer system.
Mr. John Hookimaw's daughter has also contacted the insurance
company to help with expenses and compensation.

Recommendations:

1) *We recommend that INAC and the First Nation find accommodation for
Mr. Hookimaw and his family at the earliest opportunity.*
2) *For a long term solution, it is recommended that INAC provides funding
for a Sewer Servicing study which would take into account population
growth, and land-use development, including the impact of DeBeers
occasional excess sewage load.*
3) *The OFNTSC would work with the Mushkegowuk Council Technical
Services.*

OFNTSC Contact: Derrick Kamanga, P.Eng at OFNTSC, 416-651-1443 or our
Branch Manager; Mr. Irving Leblanc, P.Eng

Appendix Two

Dr. Fricker's Template for Successful Water Projects

Given the track record of bureaucracy, it is clear that First Nations and rural community leaders must carefully tender their water treatment projects. To ensure an effective system, IBROM or otherwise, they will need to establish the boundaries by which they accept proposals.

I asked Dr. Colin Fricker for his input and direction when communities are tendering proposals for building new, or retrofitting existing, water treatment plants. Here is his recommended template for all communities, Indigenous or rural.

- That initial requests for proposals include a scientific analysis of the raw source water as well as the desired standards/levels of the finished treated water expected to be produced from the proposed system.

- That the finished treated water should meet, or exceed, specified national or international guidelines or regulations.

- That exceptional deteriorations in raw water quality that make it impossible for contractors to adequately produce the required treated water quality must be identified in the proposal.

- That successful proposals must guarantee effectiveness (that is, meeting all parameters of current guidelines and/or regulations), not just at completion, but for up to one year following the system being activated. And that payment of, perhaps, 10 to 20 percent be withheld until that is confirmed.

- A legal clause stipulating that at minimum a partial payment should be withheld to protect a community from ineffective systems being built.

- That proposals requiring the use of any chemicals must be reduced and explained.

- If an IBROM system is selected, that it be constructed with Filtralite Media. An alternative medium can be substituted only if the performance is demonstrated to meet or exceed that of Filtralite and be documented in the proposal.

Appendix Three

Communities with IBROM Water Treatment Systems

Here is a list of communities benefitting from the IBROM or SIBROM system as of 2018, when the SDWF stopped maintaining it. Unfortunately, it is now impossible to confirm later installations of IBROMs or SIBROMs, so this list is not comprehensive as of 2024.

- Yellow Quill First Nation, Saskatchewan, IBROM built in 2004 (rebuilt in 2008 due to fire)

- Pasqua First Nation, Saskatchewan, IBROM built in 2005

- George Gordon First Nation, Saskatchewan, IBROM built in 2005

- Whitecap Dakota First Nation, Saskatchewan, IBROM built in 2010

- Dakota Dunes Casino, Saskatchewan (Whitecap Dakota First Nation), IBROM built in 2010

- Saddle Lake Cree Nation, Alberta, first surface water IBROM, built in 2008

- Poundmaker Cree Nation, Saskatchewan, IBROM built in 2011

- Muskeg Lake Cree Nation, Saskatchewan, IBROM built in 2012

- Kawacatoose First Nation, Saskatchewan, IBROM built in 2012

- Witchekan Lake First Nation, Saskatchewan, IBROM built in 2012

- Saulteaux First Nation, Saskatchewan, IBROM built in 2013

- James Smith Cree Nation, Saskatchewan, IBROM built in 2013

- Moosomin, Saskatchewan, IBROM built in 2013

- Makwa Sahgaiehcan First Nation, Saskatchewan, IBROM built in 2014

- Shoal Lake Cree Nation, Saskatchewan, IBROM built in 2014

- Mistawasis First Nation, Saskatchewan, IBROM built in 2017

- Sturgeon Lake First Nation, Saskatchewan, IBROM built in 2016

- Kahkewistahaw First Nation, Saskatchewan, IBROM built in 2016

- Whitecap Dakota Casino Expansion, Saskatchewan, IBROM built in 2018

- Sandy Lake, Alberta, IBROM built in 2018

- Kinistin First Nation, Saskatchewan, IBROM built in 2018

- Village of Mankota, Saskatchewan, IBROM built in 2018

- Town of Craik, Saskatchewan, IBROM built in 2018

Appendix Four

Governments Responsible

I would like to look at who governed Canada during the last twenty-five years while the SDWF tried to educate these elected civil servants.[119]

Jean Chrétien was prime minister from 1993 until 2003.

Paul Martin was prime minister from 2003 until 2006.

Under these two prime ministers, and since October 1, 1966, the department responsible for First Nations communities was known as Indian Affairs and Northern Development.

Stephen Harper was prime minister from 2006 until November 3, 2015.

Effective June 13, 2011, the new title for the department became Aboriginal Affairs and Northern Development Canada (AANDC).

Justin Trudeau assumed office as Prime Minister in 2015 to present.

Several changes were made to the machinery of government to reflect the government's priorities on November 4, 2015. This was part of the creation of the new ministry. The name of the department changed from AANDC to Indigenous and Northern Affairs Canada (INAC).

On August 28, 2017, Trudeau announced the dissolution of INAC and the creation of two new departments: Indigenous Services Canada and Crown Indigenous Relations and Northern Affairs Canada. Carolyn Bennett, the new minister of Crown-Indigenous

Relations and Northern Affairs, claimed that the cabinet was "doing what the Royal Commission on Aboriginal Peoples (RCAP) asked for twenty years ago, to actually have two departments."[120]

Yes, the RCAP recommended this action based on three recurring complaints heard by the commission: that INAC is "colonial, paternalistic and resistant to change"; "its performance on Indigenous policy is inadequate"; and "it has not met treaty and claims obligations."[121] But did the INAC split address the substance of the complaints, or just make a name change? Whatever the name of this department, it remains colonial, paternalistic and resistant to change, for its performance on Indigenous policy regarding safe drinking water remains inadequate. More importantly, it has not made safe drinking water a reality for First Nations people.

Had they changed their ways as often as they changed their name, we would have been in a much better place today. This department has changed its name five times in the twenty-five years the SDWF has been active. What costs have been incurred with each name change? Why do they feel the need to change the name, but not the ineffective indifference and what I consider to be a criminal approach to serving First Nations people?

Over the past twenty-five years, Canada has seen thirteen different ministers, with an average of less than two years per minister. How can anyone fulfill their responsibilities with adequate understanding of the issues, knowledge and empathy required when there is such a steep learning curve? I see this brief time in the position as an opportunity to put blame on predecessors and avoid committing to the due diligence required for the position. Or do the civil servants run the departments and the ministers are their token ambassadors?

Shaun Loney refers to this in his book, *The Beautiful Bailout*, when he mentions: "In Ottawa today, civil servants who act like Indian Agents are fond of saying that cabinet ministers are 'migratory birds': they come, and they go. In other words, the bureaucracy knows best, and if the ministers disagree, they can be waited out."[122]

Assembly of First Nations (AFN): It must be challenging to be elected to lead the AFN. Their salary and costs are paid by the presiding government, while they must also appease those who elected them. The saying "never bite the hand that feeds you" comes to my mind.

Ovide Mercredi served two terms as National Chief from 1991 to 1997.

Phil Fontaine served his first term from 1997 to 2000.

Matthew Coon Come was National Chief from 2000 to 2003.

Phil Fontaine was re-elected in 2003 and served two terms as National Chief until 2009.

Shawn Atleo was elected to the office of National Chief in 2009 and re-elected for a second term in July 2012 and served as National Chief until 2014.

Ghislain Picard was interim National Chief from July 2014 to December 2014.

Perry Bellegarde was elected to the office of National Chief in December 2014 and re-elected in July 2018.

RoseAnne Archibald was elected as National Chief in 2021, becoming the first woman to hold this position. Sadly, in June of 2023, Archibald's historic electoral win ended in an unprecedented way—she became the first impeached National Chief. Two contentious issues seemed to have played a part in the Chiefs' decision to impeach Archibald. First, she pushed for a forensic audit into possible corruption within the AFN. She made specific accusations of a "crooked system" and "potentially ongoing" dishonest financial practices in a memo sent to Chiefs and obtained by APTN. That potential corruption involved people working within her department. Second, people in the workplace filed complaints against her. It's a sad time for First Nations women: they are far less likely to step up for these important roles when women like Archibald and Jody Wilson-Raybould leave their offices in such challenging ways.

Cindy Woodhouse of Pinaymootang First Nation in Manitoba was elected National Chief of AFN in December 2023. "My commitment to them is to advocate on behalf of all our communities and to improve life for all First Nations. That advocacy starts with accountability, transparency and dialogue. I look forward to working alongside the AFN Executive Committee on advancing our priorities in each region. There is much work to do and I am eager to get started on behalf of all our people."[123]

I invite women across Canada to join me and cheer her on.

Appendix Five

Recommended Reading

All of Hans's scientific publications that I reference in this book can be found on my website, susanblacklin.com.

Joel Bakan, *The Corporation: The Pathological Pursuit of Profit and Power* (New York, NY: Free Press, 2004).

Kate Beaton, *Ducks: Two Years in the Oil Sands* (Montreal, QC: Drawn & Quarterly, 2022).

Nadine Burke Harris, *Toxic Childhood Stress: The Legacy of Early Trauma and How to Heal* (London, UK: Bluebird, 2020).

Raymond Tony Charlie, *In the Shadow of the Red Brick Building* (Chemainus, BC: Askew Publishing, 2022).

Michelle Good, *Five Little Indians* (New York, NY: Harper Perennial, 2020).

Warren Goulding, *Just Another Indian: A Serial Killer and Canada's Indifference* (Chemainus, BC: Askew Creek Publishing, 2001).

Harold R. Johnson, *Peace and Good Order: The Case for Indigenous Justice in Canada* (Toronto, ON: McClelland & Stewart, 2023).

Shaun Loney with Will Braun, *The Beautiful Bailout: How a Social Innovation Scale-up Will Solve Government's Priciest Problems* (Altona, MB: Friesens, 2018).

Shaun Loney, *An Army of Problem Solvers* (Altona, MB: Friesens, 2016).

Darrel J. McLeod, *Mamaskatch: A Cree Coming of Age* (Madeira Park, BC: Douglas and McIntyre, 2018).

Darrel J. McLeod, *Peyakow: Reclaiming Cree Dignity* (Madeira Park, BC: Douglas and McIntyre, 2021).

Andrew Nikiforuk, *The Energy of Slaves, Oil and the New Servitude* (Vancouver, BC: Greystone Books, 2012).

Lisa Priest, *Conspiracy of Silence* (Toronto, ON: McClelland & Stewart, 1989).

Tanya Talaga, *Seven Fallen Feathers: Racism, Death, and Hard Truths in a Northern City* (Toronto, ON: House of Anansi Press, 2017).

Jesse Thistle, *From the Ashes: My Story of Being Métis, Homeless, and Finding My Way* (New York: Simon & Schuster, 2019).

Kevin P. Timoney, *Hidden Scourge: Exposing the Truth about Fossil Fuel Industry Spills* (Montreal, QC: McGill-Queens University Press, 2021).

Katherena Vermette, *The Break* (Toronto, ON: House of Anansi Press, 2016).

Appendix Six

Book Club Questions

Discussions around using rather than abusing science:

1. Why do you think the IBROM system was not embraced by the INAC?

2. Why does Canada still not have national drinking water regulations?

3. How do you feel about Indigenous people assuming total responsibility for their drinking water?

4. Do you believe drinking water quality should be the responsibility of the federal government for both Indigenous and non-Indigenous people of Canada?

Discussions around personal devotion to the cause:

1. How do you feel about the significant dedication of Dr. Hans Peterson?

2. Do you feel the stress of his convictions played a role in his early death?

3. How do you feel about the toll his work took on his family?

4. Was it an important factor to include Susan's past life to understand how this time in her life played out?

5. Can you imagine how this type of isolation might affect you?

Discussions around education:

1. First Nations were not allowed to hire lawyers or pass their own bylaws without approval from the Department of Indian Affairs until 1951. How does this information impact what you've read in *Water Confidential*?

2. How do you feel knowing how your tax dollars have been spent?

3. What shocked you most in this memoir?

4. Do you feel Truth and Reconciliation has been acted on by governments at all levels?

5. If you hold investments in Big Oil, are you rethinking these investments?

6. Who do you believe is ultimately responsible, and how do we hold them accountable?

Appendix Seven

Educator's Guide

There are many possible discussions and assignments that may unfold following reading this book in a classroom setting. To review the ideas and stories shared in *Water Confidential*, students may gather into groups, either having all groups review the same set of questions or each group is assigned their own specific questions; each group then presents their findings and results back to the class.

Below are some specific ideas for how groups may present ideas based on analysis of the information in the book, or information gathered through research inspired by this book:

- research and write a paragraph, a page, or an essay on a topic or story related to those in *Water Confidential*

- write a newspaper article, or compare how two (or more) existing articles covering a similar water-related issue demonstrate bias or present the same information in different ways

- write a letter to an MP, MLA or municipal councillor describing a current water issue

- create a podcast investigating a news story about water, or sharing personal stories related to water access

- stage a mock trial to sentence those who are at fault for unsafe drinking water

- prepare a presentation for the United Nations

The author Susan Blacklin invites teachers to submit students' work and commits to display all works submitted on her website: susanblacklin.com

Suggested discussion questions/prompts:

1. Do they [the students] perceive a difference between a Boil Water Advisory (BWA) and a Drinking Water Advisory (DWA)?

2. Discuss/compare drinking water regulations to drinking water guidelines or standards. Is it sufficient to meet drinking water guidelines set by government departments such as INAC/Indigenous Services Canada or should drinking water in Canada be required to meet or exceed the WHO standards for drinking water?

3. What would it be like to live under a boil water advisory? How time-consuming is the process of boiling all water used daily, and how much energy does it take? If they use the tap water, how do they feel about the risk and what risks are they facing?

4. Research the First Nations Drinking Water Settlement. Who can apply for compensation? How much compensation would they receive? How would they feel about receiving that amount of money for being under a drinking water advisory for one year or longer continuously? How much money do they feel would be the right amount? Is there a right amount that exists?

5. Do they know anyone who requires kidney dialysis? Do they see a correlation between safe water access issues and disproportionate rates of kidney disease? Are there other chronic health issues that could be related to water issues?

6. What would they do if they were a Health Inspector and learned about a First Nations community like Yellow Quill First Nation and their terrible drinking water?

7. Have there been any recent outbreaks of water-borne disease in Canada? If so, where, what, when, why and who was affected? Who is to blame?

8. How would they feel if they had been in Walkerton or North Battleford at the time of the contaminated drinking water? Would they feel entitled to compensation? Would they want someone else to be punished?

9. Describe what the IBROM means: Integrated Biological Reverse Osmosis Membrane; describe in their own words how the system functions; explain the benefits and/or challenges of the IBROM system.

10. Describe their thoughts about Engineers being responsible for all water treatment infrastructure and Hans's comment: "It is time to start seriously teaching biology at engineering schools".

11. What is the difference between drinking water guidelines and regulations? What would happen if speed limits were speed guidelines that were not legally enforceable?

12. Research the skills and/or roles of board members of an environmentally focussed charity.

13. Describe how they would feel if they were the children on the farms who had to travel into the city once a week to have a shower.

14. Research how the media chooses the stories that it covers. Is there a bias? Can they trust media to fairly represent issues?

15. Are there similarities between the effects of the oil sands on Alberta waters, and the effects of diamond mines on Ontario waters?

16. Do they think the Ontario First Nations Technical Services made a reasonable or fair response to the Attawapiskat First Nation when De Beers caused a sewage backup that flooded

the basement floors of several homes? Why or why not?

17. Discuss how they would be able to speak up on a crucial issue like their drinking water if they were invited to speak at the United Nations.

18. Discuss where corporate responsibility, and/or government responsibility begins and ends.

19. How do they feel about CEOs of large companies earning over $15 million per year? Is this different from athletes or celebrities earning exorbitant salaries?

20. Do oil companies have a responsibility to provide truly effective water treatment systems to all communities impacted by their waste products?

21. What emotion do they feel when reading about communities or governments building more homes or developing real estate instead of first addressing water issues in the community?

22. Research promises politicians made and whether they held to them. Either support or refute the argument that politicians mean what they say and include examples.

23. As much as this book is about the struggle for safe drinking water, it is also about the struggle that is experienced inside a family. Ask students to compare and contrast how these struggles are the same and how they are different.

24. Would they submit a claim if they were affected by a drinking water advisory and could register for it, knowing that registering for it would negate any future claims? Explain their reasoning.

25. How do students feel about the different rules to access the settlement, that what year they were born determines the amount of money to which they may be entitled?

26. Discuss a legacy left by a person they know.

Film "Downstream" and panel discussions:

www.youtube.com/watch?v=fc2voopGRKM (1 hour, 24 minutes).
Also available at susanblacklin.com

"Downstream" Lesson Plan:
www.safewater.org/operation-water-drop-listings/2016/10/30/
downstream-and-crapshoot-lesson-plans

"Downstream" Questions:
https://www.safewater.org/operation-water-drop-list-
ings/2016/10/29/questions-regarding-the-film-downstream

Answer Key for "Downstream" Questions:
https://www.safewater.org/operation-water-drop-list-
ings/2016/10/29/answer-key-for-downstream-questions-for-stu-
dents-to-answer-while-watching-the-film

Additional Resources

- Information about long-term drinking water advisories in
  First Nations communities: https://www.sac-isc.gc.ca/
  eng/1506514143353/1533317130660

- Information about short-term drinking water advisories in First
  Nations communities south of 60: https://www.sac-isc.gc.ca/
  eng/1562856509704/1562856530304

Endnotes

1   Office of the High Commissioner for Human Rights, "General Comment No. 15: The Right to Water," Article 11, I. Introduction, section 1, January 20, 2003

2   "Dr. Hans Peterson remembered for bringing safe drinking water to thousands." CBC News, October 31, 2018. https://www.cbc.ca/news/canada/saskatoon/dr-hans-peterson-remembered-for-bringing-safe-drinking-water-to-thousands-1.488582.1

3   "Long-Awaited AANDC Study Results Raise Concerns." Water Canada, July 21, 2021. https://www.watercanada.net/long-awaited-aandc-study-results-raise-concerns/

4   "Long-Awaited AANDC Study."

5   McCarthy Tétreault, "Stephanie Willsey named one of WXN's Top 100 Most Powerful Women," October 19, 2022, https://www.mccarthy.ca/en/about/news-and-announcements/stephanie-willsey-named-one-wxns-top-100-most-powerful-women.

6   "About," First Nations Drinking Water Settlement, https://firstnationsdrinkingwater.ca/index.php/about-us/.

7   Nadine Burke Harris, *Toxic Childhood Stress: The Legacy of Early Trauma and How to Heal* (London, UK: Bluebird, 2018).

8   For more detailed information and clarification on this topic, visit:https://www.safewater.org/fact-sheets-1/2017/1/23/purposeguidelinesregulations.

9   Hans Peterson, "Safe Drinking Water for Rural Saskatchewan," *Rural Councillor,* February 1, 1997.

10 Hans Peterson, "What is in the water besides water?" *Rural Councillor*, vol. 33, no. 10, December 1, 1998.

11 Peterson, "Safe Drinking Water."

12 Peterson, "Safe Drinking Water."

13 The Canadian Light Source Synchrotron became operational in 2004 for $173 million.

14 In November 2023, Health Canada claimed that diquat is a "herbicide that is deliberately applied to food crops and to water sources for weed control," so the "general Canadian population is therefore potentially exposed to diquat through food, and to a lesser extent, drinking water." The most recent available data is from 2018, which suggests that "more than 500,000 kg of diquat (as active ingredient) was sold in Canada. Very low levels of diquat have been detected in foods. Data provided by provinces and territories that monitor for diquat in source and drinking water indicate that levels of diquat are below the detection limit." Under "Health Effects," the website claims that repeat-dose animal studies demonstrated that diquat targeted the eyes, causing cataracts, and that it also affected the kidneys and liver. Government of Canada, "Guidelines for Canadian drinking water quality: Guideline technical document - Diquat, last modified January 1, 2022, https://www.canada.ca/en/health-canada/services/publications/healthy-living/guidelines-canadian-drinking-water-quality-guideline-technical-document-diquat.html.

15 Peterson, "Safe Drinking Water."

16 "David Schindler," science.ca, https://www.science.ca/scientists/scientistprofile.php?pID=441.

17 "New laser method could help neurosurgeons get at hard-to-reach tumours," CBC News, November 21, 2016, https://www.

cbc.ca/news/health/neuroblate-brain-surgery-1.3860572.

18   Carol Linnitt, "The Oilsands Cancer Story Part 3: The Spotlight Turns on Fort Chip Doctor," *The Narwhal*, August 17, 2014, https://thenarwhal.ca/oilsands-cancer-story-part-3-spotlight-turns-fort-chip-doctor/.

19   Hans Peterson, "Health Canada's Golden Rule." *Aboriginal Times*, June 2007.

20   "Dr. John O'Connor wins the 2021 Peter Bryce Prize," Centre for Free Expression, March 3, 2021, https://cfe.torontomu.ca/news/dr-john-oconnor-wins-2021-peter-bryce-prize.

21   Jamie Malbeuf, "Doctor who raised concerns about cancer rates downstream from oilsands wins whistleblower award," CBC News Edmonton, March 10, 2021, www.cbc.ca/news/canada/edmonton/alberta-whistleblower-fort-chipewyan-john-o-connor-1.5943389.

22   Hans expands on Dr. David Horrobin's research in his article "Schizophrenia, Cars and Algal Farming," published in the *Saskatchewan Rural Councillor* in December 1999.

23   INAC has had many names over the years. At the time of writing, INAC is called the ISC, or Indigenous Services Canada, but I've used INAC to reflect the terminology of the time period covered in this book.

24   Hans Peterson, "How Yellow Quill First Nation Ended a Nine-Year Boil Water Advisory," *Environmental Science & Engineering,* October 30, 2015, esemag.com/water/yellow-quill-first-nation/.

25   To sponsor sending a water test kit to a school or learn more about the SDWF's educational program, please visit: www.safewater.org.

26 CBC News, "Stan Koebel gets 1 year in jail, Frank 9 months house arrest," December 20, 2004, last updated December 21, 2004, www.cbc.ca/news/canada/stan-koebel-gets-1-year-in-jail-frank-9-months-house-arrest-1.485905.

27 Hans Peterson, "Walkerton - Five Years Later," *Canadian Water Treatment,* July/August 2005. www.susanblacklin.com/_files/ugd/5612d7_279d5cb1d5ac40afae07ad4cee4b0d17.pdf.

28 Peterson, "Walkerton - Five Years Later."

29 Peterson, "Walkerton - Five Years Later."

30 Hans Peterson, "First Nations Deserve Safe and Good Tasting Tap Water," *Prince Albert Grand Council Tribune,* December 2015. www.susanblacklin.com/_files/ugd/5612d7_ff3d-86faf7f34867906c19822cc9f117.pdf.

31 Peterson, "Walkerton - Five Years Later."

32 Paul Hunter, "In 2000, Walkerton's poisoned water ruined his life. He decided it was time to end it." *Toronto Star*, May 11, 2018, www.thestar.com/news/canada/in-2000-walkerton-s-poisoned-water-ruined-his-life-he-decided-it-was-time-to/article_9da32b4c-fbc3-5f98-a72f-5410983e1152.html.

33 Amanda Short, "Revisiting North Battleford's Water Crisis Twenty Years Later," *Saskatoon Star Phoenix,* May 13, 2021, thestarphoenix.com/news/saskatchewan/revisiting-north-battlefords-water-crisis-20-years-later.

34 Short, "Revisiting North Battleford."

35 "Parasites-*Cryptosporidium* (also known as 'Crypto')," Centers for Disease Control and Prevention, www.cdc.gov/parasites/crypto/index.html.

36 "Parasites."

37 Peterson, "Safe Drinking Water."

38   Jody Porter, "First Nations students get 30 per cent less funding than other children, economist says," CBC News Thunder Bay, March 14, 2016, www.cbc.ca/news/canada/thunder-bay/first-nations-education-funding-gap-1.3487822.

39   Hans Peterson, "Yellow Quill's Drinking Water Part 3: A Solution Beyond Everybody's Dreams," *Prince Albert Grand Council Tribune*, August 2015, www.susanblacklin.com/_files/ugd/5612d7_4ca5154909c248818ada182f42f0e924.pdf.

40   Matthew McClearn, "Scientist Hans Gosta Peterson Devised a Way to Clean Contaminated Water on Native Reserves," *The Globe and Mail,* November 14, 2018, www.theglobeandmail.com/canada/article-scientist-hans-gosta-peterson-devised-a-way-to-clean-contaminated/.

41   Peterson, "First Nations Deserve Safe and Good Tasting Tap Water."

42   Peterson, "Yellow Quill's Drinking Water Part 3."

43   Hans Peterson, "Yellow Quill's Drinking Water Part 4: Biology Replacing Chemistry," *Prince Albert Grand Council Tribune*, August 2015, www.susanblacklin.com/_files/ugd/5612d7_c08e4bbb398341fea69da039969d5212.pdf.

44   As quoted in "The Tale of Saddle Lake Cree Nation," Safe Drinking Water Foundation, www.safewater.org/operation-water-spirit-1/2019/4/9/grades-10-12-lesson-5-the-tale-of-saddle-lake-cree-nation.

45   Hans Peterson, "Due Diligence Equals Safe Drinking Water," *Aboriginal Times*, June 2005, www.susanblacklin.com/_files/ugd/5612d7_6320f0ca42c247b696271a03c838f80b.pdf.

46   Peterson, "Due Diligence."

47   Peterson, "Due Diligence."

48 Hans Peterson, "The Power of Biology in Drinking Water Treatment," *Canadian Water Treatment*, January/February 2008, www.susanblacklin.com/_files/ugd/5612d7_b690e-40f04384c33ad9597eedf136aa5.pdf.

49 Hans Peterson, "Chemical Limitations of Groundwater Treatment: Effective Ways of Analyzing Groundwater, and how to Determine if Chemistry Can Be Used to Purify It," *Canadian Water Treatment*, May 6, 2008, www.susanblacklin.com/_files/ugd/5612d7_37951c8867904c89a11f495526e5171b.pdf.

50 Peterson, "Chemical Limitations."

51 Peterson, "Chemical Limitations."

52 Each of these presentations can now be viewed from my website at susanblacklin.com.

53 Hans Peterson and Colin Fricker, "A Framework for Safe Drinking Water: Using science over politics in the search for safe water solutions," *Canadian Water Treatment*, November/December 2008, www.susanblacklin.com/_files/ugd/5612d7_295b-7ca483054087b06bb3697cbb84c0.pdf.

54 Peterson and Fricker, "A Framework."

55 oldenglishsheepdogs.com.

56 Andrew Nikiforuk, *Slick Water: Fracking and One Insiders Stand Against the World's Most Powerful Industry* (Vancouver, BC: Greystone Books, 2012), 111.

57 Stephen Leahy, "Fracking boom tied to methane spike in Earth's atmosphere," *National Geographic*, August 15, 2019, www.nationalgeographic.com/environment/article/fracking-boom-tied-to-methane-spike-in-earths-atmosphere.

58 Warren Goulding, *Just Another Indian: A Serial Killer and Canada's Indifference* (Chemainus, BC: Askew Creek Publishing, 2001), 211.

59 Hans Peterson, "Biological Water Treatment Discussed at UN," May/June 2005, *Canadian Water Treatment*, www.susan-blacklin.com/_files/ugd/5612d7_5433d5a0e00848c19ba3dc-6befd2a80d.pdf.

60 Peterson, "Biological Water Treatment Discussed at UN."

61 Peterson, "Biological Water Treatment Discussed at UN."

62 Peterson, "First Nations Deserve Safe and Good Tasting Tap Water."

63 Mark Blackburn, "De Beers Decision to Dump Sewage into Attawapiskat Played Role in Current Housing Crisis," *APTN National News*, December 13, 2011, www.aptnnews.ca/national-news/de-beers-decision-to-dump-sewage-into-attawapiskat-played-role-in-current-housing-crisis/.

64 See Appendix One for the memo.

65 According to the *APTN National News*, a report run by the engineers from the Ontario First Nations Technical Service claimed that the pump does not have "overload protection. This is an extremely risky way to run a pump." Blackburn, "De Beers Decision to Dump Sewage."

66 Blackburn, "De Beers Decision to Dump Sewage."

67 Quoted in Peterson, "Biological Water Treatment Discussed at UN."

68 Peterson, "Biological Water Treatment Discussed at UN."

69 Hans Peterson, Roberta Neapetung, Robert Pratt, Anthony Steinhauer, "Development of Effective Drinking Water Treatment Processes for Small Communities with Extremely Poor Quality Water on the Canadian Prairie," *Canadian Society of Environmental Biologists*, vol. 64, no. 1, Spring 2007, static1.squarespace.com/static/58f044a429687fbef7b-

2c576/t/590270e6db29d632812ea739/1493332204669/De-velopmentofEffectiveDrinkingWaterTreatmentProcessesforS-mallCommunitieswithExtremelyPoorQualityWater.pdf.

70 "History," Town of Swan Hills, www.townofswanhills.com/community/about-us/history.

71 Darcy Henton, "Liability for Swan Hills hazardous waste plant clean-up keeps growing," *Calgary Herald,* July 26, 2015, cal-garyherald.com/news/politics/liability-for-swan-hills-haz-ardous-waste-plant-clean-up-keeps-growing.

72 Paul Belanger, "Study of Human Health Impacts in the Oil Sands Area Denied for Decades," March 13, 2023, https://static1.squarespace.com/static/6014527b90b10920133c-710b/t/640f160e453cb94f9788fba6/1678710286638/HUMAN+HEALTH+IMPACTS_FINAL_Mar13_2023.docx+%281%29.pdf.

73 Keepers of the Water are "First Nations, Métis, Inuit, environ-mental groups, concerned citizens, and communities working together for the protection of water, air, land, and all living things within the Arctic Ocean Drainage Basin." Jesse Cardi-nal and Paul Belanger, "Keepers of the Water Delegation to At-tend the 2023 Dene Nation Water Summit," March 13, 2023, https://www.keepersofthewater.ca/news/denewatersummit.

74 Cardinal and Belanger, "Keepers of the Water Delegation."

75 Cardinal and Belanger, "Keepers of the Water Delegation."

76 Belanger, "Study of Human Health Impacts."

77 Cardinal and Belanger, "Keepers of the Water Delegation."

78 Belanger, "Study of Human Health Impacts."

79 The Canadian Press, "Royal Bank the No. 1 financier of fossil fuel development in the world, new report finds," April 13, 2023, www.cbc.ca/news/business/royal-bank-oil-and-gas-1.6809011.

80 Mark Burgess, "McKay tops bank CEO pay as strong earnings lead to compensation bump," March 8, 2022, last updated November 9, 2023, www.advisor.ca/industry-news/industry/mckay-tops-bank-ceo-pay-as-strong-earnings-lead-to-compensation-bump/.

81 Shaun Loney with Will Braun, *The Beautiful Bailout: How a Social Innovation Scale-up Will Solve Government's Priciest Problems* (Altona, MB: Friesens, 2018).

82 Nikiforuk, *The Energy of Slaves*, quoted in frontmatter.

83 Quoted in Joel Bakan, *The Corporation: The Pathological Pursuit of Profit and Power* (New York, NY: Free Press, 2004), 33.

84 "Oilsands Tailings Ponds Kill More Ducks," CBC News, October 26, 2010, www.cbc.ca/news/canada/edmonton/oilsands-tailings-ponds-kill-more-ducks-1.934577.

85 Kate Beaton, *Ducks: Two Years in the Oil Sands* (Montreal, QC: Drawn and Quarterly, 2022).

86 Peterson, "Walkerton: Five Years Later."

87 "Kashechewan: Water Crisis in Northern Ontario," CBC News, November 9, 2006, www.cbc.ca/news2/background/aboriginals/kashechewan.html.

88 Sarah J. Pol, "The 2005 Kashechewan Water Crisis as a One-Time Disaster and Ongoing Crisis," *Global Health: Annual Review*, vol. 1, no. 5, July 2020.

89 Hans Peterson, "The Drinking Water Saga Continues," *Aboriginal Times,* January 2006.

90 Goulding, *Just Another Indian*, 75.

91 Darrel J. McLeod, *Mamaskatch: A Cree Coming of Age* (Madeira Park: Douglas & McIntyre, 2018), 211.

92 Peterson, "First Nations Deserve Safe and Good Tasting Tap Water."

93 Hans Peterson, "Clean Drinking Water: British Columbia and the Tsunami," *Canadian Water Treatment,* March/April 2005, www.susanblacklin.com/_files/ugd/5612d7_a9ff7debfb-3c475689d5f861a336650d.pdf.

94 Jody Wilson-Raybould, "My Time in cabinet showed me how far we still had to go as a country," *The Globe and Mail,* September 18, 2021, updated September 20, 2021, www.theglobe-andmail.com/opinion/article-my-time-in-cabinet-showed-me-how-far-we-still-had-to-go-as-a-country/.

95 Sven Peterson and James Gibson, "In the Absence of Regulations: The Drinking Water Situation in First Nations Communities," *Canadian Water Treatment*, July/August, 2008.

96 Peterson and Gibson, "In the Absence of Regulations."

97 Peterson and Gibson, "In the Absence of Regulations."

98 Quoted in Peterson and Gibson, "In the Absence of Regulations."

99 McClearn, "Scientist Hans Gosta Peterson."

100 "The Team," The Safe Drinking Water Foundation, www.safedrinkingwaterteam.org/the-team.

101 Email correspondence with author, 2023.

102 Email correspondence with author, 2023.

103 Hans Peterson, "Solutions a must for water woes," *Aboriginal Times,* November/December 2006, www.susanblacklin.com/_files/ugd/5612d7_b145da4e79a746528d6d505cb-e49cd71.pdf.

104 Hans Peterson, "Unpredictable water standards: Current water treatment guidelines don't prepare for the future," *ReNew Canada*, October 2005.

105 The WHO's Guidelines for Drinking-Water Quality can be found here: https://www.who.int/teams/environment-climate-change-and-health/water-sanitation-and-health/water-safety-and-quality/drinking-water-quality-guidelines.

106 This comment was provided to me under the condition that the source remain anonymous. The next two paragraphs have been written using numerous anonymous sources; I'm grateful to all of you.

107 Email correspondence with author, 2023.

108 "Our Mission," Saskatchewan First Nations Water Association, sfnwa.ca/mission.

109 Anonymous source, in communication with the author, 2023.

110 Italics added for emphasis.

111 Olivia Stefanovich, "Feds Introduce Bill to Set Drinking Water Standards in First Nations," CBC News, December 11, 2023, www.cbc.ca/news/politics/ottawa-bill-protect-first-nations-drinking-water-1.7055352?cmp=rss.

112 The settlement aims to address Canada's failure to take all reasonable steps to make sure First Nations communities have adequate access to safe drinking water. Discover more information about the settlement here: https//firstnationsdrinkingwater.ca.

113 Italics added for emphasis.

114 Raymond Tony Charlie, *In the Shadow of The Red Brick Building* (Chemainus, BC: Askew Creek Publishing, 2022), 72.

115 It is called "Developing Laws and Regulations for First Nations Drinking Water and Wastewater: Engagement 2022 to 2023," and its status is closed at the time of this writing. https://www.rcaanc-cirnac.gc.ca/eng/1330528512623/1698157290139.

116 "Safe Water for First Nations," The Council of Canadians, https://canadians.org/fn-water/.

117 Email correspondence with the author, 2024.

118 This paragraph has been excerpted and paraphrased from my article "My Garden of Creative Inspiration" in *Sage-ing with Creative Spirit, Grace and Gratitude: The Journal of Creative Aging,* no. 4, Spring 2000, 19–21.

119 Sources for this appendix include "Prime Ministers of Canada," Parliament of Canada, lop.parl.ca/sites/ParlInfo/default/en_CA/People/primeMinisters; "Privy Council Office," Government of Canada, www.canada.ca/en/privy-council.html; and "Our History," Assembly of First Nations, afn.ca/about-us/our-history/.

120 Veldon Coburn, "The Dismantling of INAC," *Policy Options*, September 6, 2017, policyoptions.irpp.org/magazines/september-2017/the-dismantling-of-indigenous-and-northern-affairs-canada/.

121 Coburn, "The Dismantling of INAC."

122 Loney, *The Beautiful Bailout.*

123 "Cindy Woodhouse Elected as National Chief of Assembly of First Nations," Assembly of First Nations, December 7, 2023, afn.ca/all-news/press-releases/cindy-woodhouse-elected-as-national-chief-of-assembly-of-first-nations/.

About the Author

Susan Blacklin was born near London, UK, and later moved to Canada. While living in Saskatchewan, she supported her now late ex-husband, Dr. Hans Peterson, in founding the Safe Drinking Water Foundation; together, they devoted fifteen years of their lives to bringing safe drinking water to First Nations and rural communities. Susan retired to Vancouver Island, where she now pursues her writing, painting, and gardening. *Water Confidential* is her first book.